The Indictment

THE INDICTMENT

Prosecuting the Chinese Communist Party & Friends
for Crimes against America, China, and the World

by Frank J. Gaffney
with Dede Laugesen

Foreword by Steve Bannon

For the Committee on the Present Danger: China

Skyhorse Publishing

Skyhorse Publishing books may be purchased in bulk at special discounts for sales promotion, corporate gifts, fund-raising, or educational purposes. Special editions can also be created to specifications. For details, contact the Special Sales Department, Skyhorse Publishing, 307 West 36th Street, 11th Floor, New York, NY 10018 or info@skyhorsepublishing.com.

Skyhorse® and Skyhorse Publishing® are registered trademarks of Skyhorse Publishing, Inc.®, a Delaware corporation.

Visit our website at www.skyhorsepublishing.com.

10 9 8 7 6 5 4 3 2 1

Library of Congress Cataloging-in-Publication Data is available on file.

Webinar art by Oleg Atbashian
Interior Design by JP Watson, Valley House Books
Jacket design by Brian Peterson

Print ISBN: 978-1-64821-004-4
Ebook ISBN: 978-1-64821-003-7

Printed in the United States of America

Phone: (202) 835-9077 | Email: info@securefreedom.org
For more information, please see securefreedom.org

Freedom is never more than one generation away from extinction. We didn't pass it on to our children in the bloodstream. The only way they can inherit the freedom we have known is if we fight for it, protect it, defend it and then hand it to them with the well-thought lessons of how they in their lifetime must do the same.

And if you and I don't do this, then you and I may well spend our sunset years telling our children and our children's children what it once was like in America when men were free.

— Ronald Reagan, 1961 speech,
"Encroaching Control"

Dedication

To my beloved wife, Marisol, and to our children and our children's children. May this book help ensure that they all know *firsthand* what it is like to live in America when everyone is free.

Acknowledgements

I want to express my deep appreciation to all those who made *The Indictment* possible. They include: Brian Kennedy, the superb Chairman of the Committee on the Present Danger: China and one of its sponsors as President of the American Strategy Group. Tommy Waller, the estimable new President and CEO of the CPDC's other sponsor, the Center for Security Policy. Dede Laugesen, the CPDC's Executive Secretary, chief cat-herder for its webinars and other products, including this book, and my right hand in pulling the best of the Committee's content together for the present use. And Oleg Atbashian, the CPDC's brilliant graphic artist and indefatigable technical maestro.

I am very grateful to others who helped distill the quotes that bring to life the various points made throughout *The Indictment*, including CPDC members Brian Kennedy, Connie Elliott, Suzanne Scholte, Bradley Thayer and Grant Newsham. And to several other colleagues at the Center for Security Policy who lent a hand in unique ways at various points, including our extraordinary Chief of Staff Morgan Wirthlin and trusty Digital Media Producer and webmaster Matthew Franklin.

Finally, I want to thank all those who participated in the production of the Committee's dozens of webinars, in some cases, repeatedly. There are too many of them to address individually here, but all of their names are listed at the back of this volume. It is my profound hope that the Congress will further tap their remarkable expertise and skills in illuminating the points we believe are vital to the proper understanding of and response to the Chinese Communist Party and its friends' war crimes against us and its other crimes against humanity elsewhere in the world.

We look forward to working with America's representatives on Capitol Hill in prosecuting the case made in this Indictment—at a minimum, in the court of public opinion—and to making the defeat of the Chinese Communist Party a decisive voting issue in 2024.

Frank J. Gaffney

Contents

FOREWORD

The Chinese Communist Party is at war with America, and has been for three decades. The CCP will likely add a kinetic component to their already successful "unrestricted warfare" techniques inflicted against the United States, in and around Taiwan, and the rest of the world. The Chinese Communists expect to win what they are making a global conflict, World War III—thanks to the American elites they have captured in every sector of our society.

These are the chilling conclusions that jump off the pages of *The Indictment: Prosecuting the Chinese Communist Party & Friends for Crimes against America, China, and the World*. They are documented by over seventy web broadcasts conducted in 2022 by the Committee on the Present Danger: China. As one of the co-founders of that group, I am overwhelmed by the hard evidence presented in these programs. Frank Gaffney and Dede Laugesen have made that impressive body of work accessible at this important moment.

The United States now has a crucial opportunity to change the course of history concerning the mortal threat we face by the Chinese Communist Party.

On 21 March 2023, as this book was going to press, President Xi Jinping and Vladimir Putin held a summit in Moscow that Xi declared would "lead to changes we haven't see in one hundred years."

Do not look away. This deadly hegemonic partnership could never have come about except for the broad swath of American and Global Elites supporting it. The election last year of a Republican majority in the U.S. House of Representatives has promised corrective action. But the action created by this wake-up call must be driven by the working people of America, Republican and Democratic citizens.

The Indictment must invigorate and inform the work of the 118th Congress' Select Committee on the Competition Between the United States and the Chinese Communist Party, the Congressional-Executive

Commission on China, and other committees of the House of Representatives.

With its nine "Charges" against the CCP for war crimes against America and humanity—the latter inflicted on the people of China and of China's captive nations (Tibet, Southern Mongolia, East Turkistan and, most recently, the territory of Hong Kong), *The Indictment's* specific recommendations in this book can streamline the process of adopting the war footing required to defend America and take down the CCP.

There is no alternative. Let me repeat; There is no alternative. The Chinese Communist Party regards this as a "zero-sum" game. Either they will realize Xi Jinping's ambition to rule and enslave the world, especially the one country in the world that stands in the way: the United States of America. Or the CCP will lose and be toppled by the Chinese people desperate to enjoy fundamental human freedoms.

This reality must inform everything we do from now on. Those of us called "Super Hawks" with regard to the Chinese Communist Party will accept no substitute for victory.

Thwarting a world order "with Chinese characteristics" is the existential challenge of our time. We must rise to that challenge as our forefathers did. Our children and our children's children must have the chance to live a free life, enjoying the liberty, prosperity, and opportunities we take for granted. *The Indictment* is a playbook, the manual, for doing just that. It is required reading across our land if America is to be saved.

Introduction

The American people have had a wake-up call. One of the Chinese Communist Party's high-altitude spy balloons spent over a week wafting unimpeded over some of America's most sensitive military sites. Besides the threat arising from such surveillance and the possibility that this aerial vehicle's payload might include something even more dangerous than espionage gear, the failures of the U.S. government initially to disclose the balloon's violation of our sovereign air space and then to terminate it was deeply unsettling to millions of our countrymen and women.

That reaction would be all the more pronounced if the American people understood that Beijing's balloon belligerence is but a prime, if microcosmic, example of a far larger problem: For decades, the Chinese Communist Party (CCP) has used every means available—thus far, short of open military conflict—to pursue two overarching goals:

1. achieving the complete, totalitarian control of its own population and those of every other country in the world, and

2. effecting the destruction of the United States as the principal impediment to China's restoration to its rightful place globally, namely as the "middle kingdom" ruling "all under heaven."

The balloon episode, and the official U.S. response to it, also showcased the success of one of the CCP's principal techniques for achieving these objectives: the Chinese Communists' "elite capture" evident with respect to President Joe Biden, his family and many of his subordinates, among myriad others.

For millennia, Chinese emperors and warlords routinely utilized corruption of their adversaries' elites to obtain, and maintain, dominion over others. Going back at least to Sun Tzu's time, the practice of *winning without fighting* has been a mainstay of such rulers' strategies The Chinese Communist Party has elevated these practices to an art form, enabling it to make huge strides in undermining this country without firing a shot and advancing the worldwide hegemony to which it has long aspired.

Unfortunately, with the apparent completion of Xi Jinping's consolidation of power at home, his unprecedented build-up of the People's Liberation Army and his effective colonization (to varying degrees) of roughly 147 other nations via the so-called Belt and Road Initiative (BRI), the Chinese Communist Party is now poised to achieve its two objectives: Through a combination of cooption, coercion and the threat and/or the use of brute force—the realization of what Xi calls "The China Dream" is no longer unthinkable.

Of particular concern is the inexorable, and accelerating, progress the Chinese Communist Party is making towards replicating worldwide what has been aptly called "the Digital Gulag" it has installed at home. Techniques advanced by the CCP under the guise of its "social credit system" are being embraced and proliferated by Beijing's friends elsewhere, including: the globalist oligarchs of the World Economic Forum (WEF); the Director General of the World Health Organization, Dr. Tedros Ghebreyesus; the conniving Muslim Brotherhood and its Organization of Islamic Cooperation; and another Chinese controlled asset, Joe Biden, together with many fellow travelers in his administration and among America's CCP-captured elites. In addition to exporting the Party's social credit system, these forces are collaborating in the creation and imposition of: universal vaccine passports; new authorities for Ghebreyesus to declare pandemics and compulsorily mandate national responses to them; and Central Bank Digital Currencies (CBDC).

Those who recognize that Xi Jinping's China Dream—a formula for a global totalitarian hegemony "with Chinese characteristics"—would unmistakably be a *nightmare* for anyone who loves freedom are obliged to do two things, *starting immediately*: 1) Urgently produce an honest appraisal of the damage done by the CCP's belligerence and its associated war crimes against us and the Party's criminal mistreatment of its own people. And, 2) address how the Chinese Communist Party can yet be *defeated*. Execution of that strategy must begin at once if we are to thwart our mortal enemy's determined bid to crush liberty and institute a terrifying "new world order" directed and enforced from Beijing.

The United States' 2022 elections have given a Republican majority in the House of Representatives a platform for conducting such an evaluation, and determining and adopting the corrective actions that are now required to prevent the CCP's enslavement and/or destruction of America, its friends and allies and everyone else.

To facilitate such an unvarnished examination, the Committee on the Present Danger: China (CPDC) and its sponsors, the Center for Security Policy (CSP) and the American Strategy Group (ASG), have conducted in the closing months of 2022 a comprehensive program of some 70 webinars involving more than 150 individual commentaries, analyses and answers to probing questions concerning two broad topics:

The nature, manifestations and impacts of the CCP's decades-long, self-described "Unrestricted Warfare" against America—both the pre-kinetic kind that continues to this day and the full-on violent sort now in prospect; and

The sources and extent of the assistance rendered by *America's own elites* who have—whether as individuals, corporations or other entities—systematically helped the CCP weaponize elements of the U.S. business, finance, media, culture, academic and governmental sectors against their own country.

We have drawn heavily on the lightly edited quotes from many of the participants in these webinars and other of our programs to illuminate and embellish key points made throughout the text.

In addition to the powerful body of work represented by these webinars and the inputs they have elicited from many of the most knowledgeable, articulate and courageous subject matter experts on Communist China, former government officials and other national security professionals, the CPDC and its sponsors have helped produce a wealth of broadcast interviews, public events and an authoritative new book entitled, *The CCP is at War with America*.

Drawing upon all this content, the present book, *The Indictment*, identifies nine "charges" that can and should be pressed against the Chinese Communist Party and its American enablers. It is our hope that congressional investigators, executive branch officials, journalists and the public at large will review these charges, draw upon the accompanying highlights of the Committee's webinars and, as needed, utilize the embedded QR codes to examine the webinars in their entirety for a surpassingly important and extremely urgent purpose: Assessing the guilt of the Chinese Communist Party for unimaginably horrific crimes, past, present and prospective, against its own people and countless others, including ours—the essential first step towards holding accountable and taking down the CCP and its friends.

PART I

The Charges against the Chinese Communist
Party (CCP)

Charge 1:
The CCP Has Perpetrated Crimes against the People of China and Its Captive Nations

Any indictment of the CCP must begin with its very first, most horrific *and ongoing* crimes against humanity—namely, those that it has inflicted on the population of the People's Republic of China.

For over 70 years, the Chinese people have been relentlessly subjected to a range of barbarous outrages including: mass starvation, forced migration, rape, torture, industrial-grade organ harvesting, the persecution of religious communities on an unimaginably vast scale, slave labor, millions of political prisoners and others unlawfully incarcerated, forced abortions and genocide.

One of the most brutal expressions of this CCP-sponsored practice of crimes against humanity was Mao's "Cultural Revolution" and the "People's War" he unleashed across China. As a child, Xi Van Fleet[1] was a witness to and survivor of its predations. Today, as a Chinese expatriate and naturalized American citizen, this freedom-fighter described the central impetus behind Mao's murderous campaign—which is very much operating today, as well: "I would say about the People's War, always remember communism. They depend on…permanent revolution or permanent struggle. Struggle against someone. It is always someone, either an enemy within or an enemy without. They depend on that to maintain their power."

This permanent struggle is currently being manifested in what has been officially recognized by the U.S. government under both Presidents Trump[2] and Biden[3] as "genocide" against the Uyghur and other Muslim minorities of the Captive Nation historically known as East Turkistan but dubbed Xinjiang by the Chinese Communists who invaded and conquered it in 1949.

One of East Turkistan's most articulate champions in the West is Julie Milsap, Government Relations Officer at the Uyghur Human Rights Project. She warns[4]:

What is happening to the Uyghurs is an illustration of the vision that China has for the world. Why the Uyghurs? Why are they wiping out the Uyghurs? Because to be perfectly honest, there's a moral foundation here that they don't have in the rest of China. And this again, brings this highlighted concept of justice. We might say that's a very democratic or Western concept, but justice is very important here. This is a nonexistent concept in China. [Justice] is not emphasized.

What is emphasized is "harmony" and harmony is a word that can be very easily manipulated by the state to mean "not causing trouble," "living peacefully." What does it mean to live peacefully? Does that mean the absence of trouble is the absence of struggle? But, because good and evil exist, there will always be struggle. And so, if we don't have that concept of justice, society is empty and terrifying, to be honest.

This is why China is a threat to the world because their system allows the worst parts of human nature to flourish, and the best parts of human nature are stifled.

And so, this is incredibly dangerous. And we need to grasp that in the Western world. We need to not be so naive as to continue to think that China can be a reliable partner on anything. It has been proven time and time again: They will never cooperate with the West except where there's a win-win for them—both wins going to China....

The United States has continued to buy into this naive belief that they can just talk enough at China and bring them to the table as a good faith actor. This is ideologically motivated. It's not motivated by the same factors that we view things within the West. It's not even pragmatic per se. It is ideological.

Lest anyone think such horrors cannot be inflicted outside of China, Se Hoon Kim, the Director of the Committee on the Present Danger: China's Captive Nation Coalition, observes, it already has[5]:

["Death Camps"] is a real term that should wake up everybody. And I say this because these camps not only are literally killing

people, but they're also taking out their organs and they're also taking their hair.[6]

These facilities not only kill people directly, but [such institutionalized repression] also destroys every aspect of what makes us human beings. The Uyghurs, Uzbeks, Kyrgyz and all other people of East Turkistan that are being brutalized in these camps....These people are not even considered as human beings, just like how we saw in the Holocaust where Jews were considered non-human. They were beings that could be disposed of at any point. And in a modern context, these Uyghurs are now viewed as just body parts that can be sold, particularly to Arab nations. We're seeing cases of individuals from nations like Saudi Arabia coming to demand ["halal"] organs from Muslims.[7] And...at the same time, it's a camp just like the camps in Dachau and Auschwitz.

I'm not saying that the two situations are by any means equal, but I will say that the term "never again" is becoming, unfortunately a myth. And if it continues, we may see something that is even worse than the Holocaust taking its place because of the advanced technologies. But more importantly, world governments like our own government, and especially as we've seen with [then-UN Human Rights Commissioner] Michelle Bachelet, conforming and normalizing brutal persecution of the most vulnerable people—particularly the people of East Turkistan.[8]

The diabolical advanced technologies to which Kim refers include an Orwellian instrument that now greatly facilitates the CCP's whole-of-society repression: the "Social Credit System."[9]

This weapon for unprecedented tyranny is the natural evolution of the Chinese Communist Party's decades of totalitarian oppression married with 21st Century means of achieving real-time surveillance, control and enslavement of entire populations. Such techniques include: face- and gait-recognition, millions of video cameras and other means of Big Data collection, quantum computing, artificial intelligence and advanced algorithms.

And particularly ominous is the fact that this system is now not only in use throughout China. It is being increasingly exported around the world.

China expert Dr. Bradley Thayerm PhD,[10] cited a prominent African leader to capture the essential characteristic of the Chinese Communist Party's hegemonism in practice[11]:

> *I was always struck by a great Zambian politician named Guy Scott, [who], reflecting on China's influence in Africa, including his own country of Zambia, said, "We've had bad people before. The whites were bad. The Indians were worse. But the Chinese are worst of all in terms of their exploitation of the Zambian people, of their abuse of the people, and the inability to recognize the Zambians as humans, rather than in essence, being a commodity for consumption and to serve at the behest of the Chinese Communist Party."[12]*

> *Guy Scott's comments really [are] the heart of the issue, which is the dehumanization. Whether it's Muslim peoples, Kazakhs, Tartars or Uyghurs in East Turkistan, whether it's Mongols, whether it's Manchus, whether it's Tibetans or other oppressed minorities or the diaspora abroad, the Chinese Communist Party [insists] on crushing dissent, even in the diaspora population, reaching into the United States, Canada, every country around the world to crush these individuals.*

Here's the key point: Any regime that treats its own people so badly will not treat others, *including ours*, better. That's really important to understand because, as we will discuss in connection with Charge 2, the unmistakable aspiration of the Chinese Communist Party under its current emperor, Xi Jinping, is to control the world so that the CCP can, in fact, subject *everyone* to at least as relentless repression as it imposes on its own people.

The only real impediment to the Chinese Communist Party realizing that frightening ambition is the United States. Consequently, the CCP is determined to destroy this country as a necessary precondition to becoming the world's hegemon. As the next Charge will make clear, we cannot afford to be under any illusion about the fact that the regime in

Beijing is at war with America. That discussion will, in turn, set the stage for our review in subsequent Charges of how the Chinese Communists have long used pre-kinetic unrestricted warfare techniques in their bid to prevail in that war—and may now be poised to employ the violent kind of warfare to finish us off.

As we turn to those topics, bear in mind a further warning that the intent of the nightmare that is Xi Jinping's China Dream is to extend tyranny "with Chinese characteristics" far beyond China and its Captive Nations. As Zubayra Shamseden, China Outreach Coordinator of the Uyghur Human Rights Project in Zambia, put it[13]:

> *Whatever is happening to [Uyghurs] today will probably happen to anyone, anyone in the world, because… it's happening already in mainland China….What's happening in Hong Kong is quite similar to what's happening to us. Taiwan is next. And Africa right now, I mean, it's already [a] Chinese colony….*
>
> *What China's government sees and values is completely… different than what we value as a human being, as a believer, as a people who value democracy, freedom and human rights because there is no such a thing in China's government's mind—and, unfortunately, all the beliefs of China's people's mind because they have been ingrained in the mind for so many years from birth. That ideology that they have in mind is just horrible.*
>
> *If all those people grow up, and grow up with that, it brings a huge nightmare to the world.*
>
> *So, we have to stop China. That's what I would say to the world.*

CHARGE 2:
The CCP Is at War with America

Since Mao's time, the Communist Party has been patiently, but relentlessly, pursuing the United States' downfall, clearing the way for China's restoration to its rightful place as "the Middle Kingdom," "the center of the universe," "ruling all under heaven." Its personnel actually killed Americans while fighting alongside our adversaries in Korea and Vietnam. The CCP also mounted a number of "wars of national liberation" around the world aimed at destabilizing and removing governments friendly to America and replacing them with regimes allied with the Communist bloc.

When the Soviet Union was defeated in the Cold War, China's then-leader, Deng Xiaoping, resolved that a new Cold War between the United States and China was commencing—and that China would win it.

Toward that end, Deng promulgated a policy that came to be known as the "Hide and Bide" strategy, whereby the government in Beijing would profess that China wants nothing more than to become part of the community of nations, ostensibly to improve the lot of its people.[14]

The West was encouraged to believe that, as the PRC became richer, it would inevitably conform to the existing, so-called rules-based order and become, well, more like us.

As the Director of Britain's MI-5 intelligence service, Ken McCallum, pointed out on July 6, 2022, in a joint press conference with his American counterpart, FBI Director Christopher Wray, that is not what happened[15]:

> *The widespread Western assumption that growing prosperity within China and increasing connectivity with the West would automatically lead to greater political freedom has been shown to be plain wrong. But the Chinese Communist Party is interested in our democratic, media and legal systems. Not to emulate them, sadly, but to use them for its gain.*

In fact, Deng's plan was designed from the get-go to mask the CCP's true intentions for global domination and to patiently use the West to strengthen China so that it could, in due course, destroy the United States and control the rest of the world.

Interestingly, at about the same time that Deng launched this devious strategy, he reportedly tasked the Chinese Communist Party's biological warfare program with an ambitious and unimaginably horrific goal: depopulating the United States so that it could be taken over and colonized by China.[16, 17] (We will have more to say about this agenda with respect to Charge 4 concerning China's biological attack against America and the rest of the world.)

In 1999, the mask Deng put into place to conceal the Chinese Communist Party's true, malevolent purpose was allowed to slip a bit. Two senior colonels in the People's Liberation Army—both of whom went on to become general officers—published a book entitled *Unrestricted Warfare*.[18] It laid out in considerable detail China's strategy for using "non-kinetic" means of waging war against our nation and what was then a far-superior U.S. military. We will address in subsequent Charges how this strategy was assiduously executed. For the present, suffice it to say that the cumulative impact of such warfare has been devastating for this country, especially given the help the CCP received from American elites in conducting it against us. As we shall document in the following Charges, the unprovoked acts of unrestricted warfare constitute war crimes against America.

In May 2019, twenty years after the publication of *Unrestricted Warfare*, the Chinese Communist Party became considerably more forthright about their true intentions by declaring a "People's War" against the United States. They did this not in some secret internal directive, but in the Party's prime propaganda outlet: *People's Daily*.[19]

An expert in ideological and political warfare, Connie Elliott,[20] explains what the Chinese Communists mean by that term:

> *People's War is a form of war [that] is a struggle between two or more entities for control of people, resources or territory. It is characterized by violence or a threat of violence. Either physical or psychological. Mao developed this concept of people's war. It is the structure within which he goes from zero to developing what he calls "mass."*

Xi Van Fleet was a child in China who experienced and survived Mao's People's War against his domestic adversaries and Party rivals which he branded "the Cultural Revolution." Today, she is a Chinese expatriate, naturalized American and freedom-fighter who recalls the CCP's past—and continuing—warfare against its foes[21]:

> I would say about the People's War, always remember communism. [The Communists] depend on permanent revolution or permanent struggle. Struggle against someone. It is always someone, either an enemy within or an enemy without. They depend on that to maintain their power.

There is, in short, no excuse for lingering illusions about the CCP's intentions towards this country—or any basis for treating it as other than our mortal enemy.

That is especially the case insofar as the evidence continues to accumulate that the CCP has been steadily preparing for the kind of kinetic warfare that was not an option in 1999. Those preparations are the more ominous for their being rooted in a "whole-of-society" approach towards Chinese mobilization, guided by a doctrine Xi's regime has dubbed "civil-military fusion."[22]

Career U.S. undercover intelligence operative Charles "Sam" Faddis detailed[23] why this approach poses such a threat to America:

> The Chinese have this official policy of civil-military fusion. Which, quite frankly, is just what any commonsense[-minded] American understands. There is no distinction between the Chinese Communist Party and private enterprise, or between the Chinese military and private enterprise. The Chinese Communist Party is a totalitarian, thuggish entity. It runs the country. It takes whatever it wants. It does whatever it wants.
>
> If you are a Chinese company, you will do whatever the Chinese government tells you to do. You will give them whatever information they want. And if you have access to American technology vis a vis some sort of joint venture or cooperation with or business dealing with an American company, well, if the

CCP wants that, the CCP gets it. I mean, there's no way to resist that. You do what you're told.

This reality renders suicidal U.S. private sector and governmental efforts to invest in, share dual-use technology among or otherwise do business with Chinese entities. Yet, such efforts largely continue apace, despite the growing prospect of violent hostilities.

Among the evidence that the CCP is preparing for actual conflict against us is a videotaped high-level planning session in Guangdong Province on May 14, 2022,[24] whose stated mission was to prepare China's largest and wealthiest province for the transition "from normal to war." Dr. Bradley Thayer, China Policy Director for the Center for Security Policy explained the significance of this exercise[25]:

> *[First, it suggests that the Chinese Communists] believe that events are moving in their direction and that's quite alarming for the United States, its allies and all states that seek to resist the Chinese Communist Party. A second significant element of this for China is their idea of a pre-crisis action.*
>
> *Normally, we think in international politics or events that there's peacetime, there's crisis and there's war. The Chinese have a notion of pre-crisis, where they seek to act in peacetime to set the stage for a surprise attack to be directed that would lead to a crisis or that would lead to a conflict. So, we're seeing emphasis that they are in a pre-crisis situation. They are taking actions, mobilizations to which we're not responding as we should.*

Indeed, the United States has no remotely comparable mobilization effort underway. For that matter, most U.S. policymakers seem unaware even of the extent of the one being mounted by the CCP. As author and China authority Gordon G. Chang[26] puts it: "Is America at war with China? No. But is China at war with America? Yes."

One former American military leader, Lieutenant General William "Jerry" Boykin, U.S. Army (Ret.) is under no illusion about the Chinese Communist Party, its intentions and its actions[27]:

> *What's important about [The CCP is at War with America] is that it makes very clear what China's intentions are for America.*

And [they are] not good. They want to dominate the world politically, economically, militarily in all aspects. . . . And, America is rolling over and giving them an opportunity to succeed.

In short, at least since May 2019, if not long before (as suggested by the publication of *Unrestricted Warfare* two decades previously), we have been on notice that the Chinese Communist Party is, indeed, at war with the United States. Yet, we have persisted in treating the CCP as a partner with whom we can do business, both literally and diplomatically, geopolitically and through mutually respectful and benign military interactions.

Today, we are unprepared to face not only the combined effects of the CCP's twenty-plus years of relentless Unrestricted Warfare pursued via the techniques outlined in the following seven Charges. We must confront, as well, the distinct prospect of a little-to-no warning, and possibly devastating, attack by the CCP against not only Taiwan, but also U.S. allies in the region and even American assets, personnel and territory.

It follows that, since the CCP is at war with us, any American aiding and abetting the Chinese Communists, whether directly or indirectly, is betraying our country.

Everyone in America, and most especially their elected representatives, must, therefore, be informed and clear-eyed about these facts—and thereby equipped to hold the CCP accountable for this and the other Charges in this Indictment that must be prosecuted in the court of public opinion and via the policies of the U.S. government.

Charge 3:
The CCP Has Captured America's Elite and Is Using It to Take Us Down

Throughout China's history, emperors and war lords have used corruption to weaken, subdue and ensure the submission of rivals. Frequently, the targets have been compromised and control over them obtained through the enriching of their offspring or other family members.

This practice accords with principles of warfare taught by the ancient Chinese strategist, Sun Tzu, including:

> *1. Generally in War the best policy is to take a state intact; to ruin it is inferior to this. 2. To capture the enemy's army is better than to destroy it; to take intact a battalion, a company or a five-man squad is better than to destroy them. And 3. For to win one hundred victories in one hundred battles is not the acme of skill. To subdue the enemy without fighting is the acme of skill.*[28]

The Chinese Communist Party has raised the practice of subversive corruption of its enemies' leadership so as to improve the chances of winning without fighting to an art form through its multibillion-dollar-a-year investment in what it calls "elite capture." Peter Schweizer, the best-selling author of *Red Handed: How China Wins by Making American Elites Rich*[29], observes[30]:

> *China has a very explicit strategy that they basically call elite capture, which is designed to provide financial and other inducements to capture elites to effectively do their bidding.... In some instances, the CCP officials aren't necessarily looking for state secrets. They're simply looking for elites who are going to advance their interests.*

Various entities are utilized for this purpose including: Chinese intelligence; the CCP's United Front Work Department; the PRC's diplomatic corps; and businesses that, pursuant to the Party's doctrine of "civil-military fusion" act as extensions of the government's recruitment, entrapment, coercion and collection techniques.

Steven Mosher was the first Western social scientist to be allowed to do research in Communist China and his deep understanding of the Party, its misrule and its ambitions to dominate the planet in time informed a key insight[31]:

> Back in the late nineties. I worked with the Cox Commission investigating the corruption and the espionage of China and the corruption in the Clinton campaign. At that time, there were an estimated 8,000 front organizations run by various PRC intelligence services....I think here of Stalin's remark that quantity has a quality all of its own. The quantity, the sheer scale of the effort of Chinese espionage is astonishing.

As Trevor Loudon—the author of *Enemies Within*[32] and a man who is arguably the West's preeminent authority on Communist penetration and subversion—has observed, one of the appeals of "elite capture" to the CCP is its sheer cost-effectiveness.[33] For a fraction of the outlay involved in waging economic warfare against a country like the United States, to say nothing of a decisive military conflict, the Chinese Communists can buy, control and benefit hugely from the subversive service rendered by leaders in America's business, finance, academic, media and government sectors.

> If you were Xi Jinping and you wanted to take down the United States, you wanted to take down—and I mean, take down physically, not just dominate economically—but if you wanted to take down this country, would you want to spend billions of dollars on a trade war that would hurt your own economy and set your own people against you, your own elites against you? Would you want to prematurely risk a multi-trillion dollar shooting war? And I say prematurely, because there will come a time when they would do this. Or would you rather spend a few billion dollars buying up American elites?

According to career CIA clandestine service officer, Charles "Sam" Faddis,[34] Chinese intelligence has clearly chosen to invest heavily in buying up our elites, among others:

What we're talking about here is something that is done very, very deliberately by the Chinese government under a whole-of-government concept. Basically, every point of contact with the Chinese government, or really any Chinese entity, is exploited for the purpose of capturing the elite of a target country. And by this point, probably every country is a target country, but certainly the United States is at the very, very top of that list.

So, very deliberately, very methodically in a very, very organized fashion, the Chinese Communist Party pursues capturing, getting their hooks into [and] controlling the elite of target countries....They're not just looking to be your friend or anything that just might be painted in some sort of neutral fashion. They want to control, manipulate and direct the elite in the United States for the purposes of having them pursue policies that are beneficial to the Chinese Communist Party. It's that straightforward. It is that blatant. And it happens on a massive, like industrial scale.

Particularly alarming is the proof provided by Hunter Biden's laptop[35] of what may be the greatest elite capture of all time. According to Sam Faddis[36], Chinese intelligence has rendered the U.S. Commander-in-Chief, Joe Biden, a "controlled asset" of the CCP:

...This is about a guy [who] gets money and whatever else he gets. And he dances to the tune that is played. Now, how that actually works face-to-face, that depends on the personalities involved. But it doesn't change the fact [that] the asset who, in this case would be Joe Biden, ultimately does what he is told to do on behalf of the people who have purchased him....That is how espionage works.

At the CIA, if your asset doesn't satisfy the criteria for being controlled, he is not an asset. He is not recognized as an asset....No professional, serious intelligence organization wants to maintain contact with an asset who will not accept being controlled, because he may be a liability because you don't know which direction he's going. You don't really know what side he's playing for.

It is difficult to overstate the dire implications of President Biden's capture by the CCP. But, if the Commander-in-Chief's status as a controlled asset of the CCP were not frightening enough, his selection of people as senior subordinates who are similarly compromised by China—whether as a result of their own or family corruption or simply out of Marxist ideological solidarity—is imperiling U.S. national security.

To pick just one example, Secretary of State Antony Blinken has longstanding ties to the Chinese Communists.[37] Notably, during his time as the president of the Penn Biden Center, the organization garnered tens of millions of dollars from anonymous Chinese sources. In exchange, in Faddis' professional judgment[38]:

> *The [Penn Biden] Center is a propaganda entity for the Chinese Communist Party. That's what it is. It spouts nothing but Chinese propaganda and rhetoric. It is not a center that studies American policy or recommends American policy or anything else. It is a center that broadcasts Chinese Communist Party propaganda directly to the U.S. government [and] influences students, influences professors, influences policymakers.*

Unfortunately, the Chinese Communist Party has succeeded in compromising not only Joe Biden and many senior members of his administration[39], but key members of Congress, as well, including the bipartisan leadership in both houses. New Zealand expatriate and internationally recognized expert on the phenomenon of "Enemies Within," Trevor Loudon, cites two illustrative examples whose damage persists to this day[40]:

> *John Conyers, a congressman from Michigan who had a fifty-year history with the Communist Party USA, was a card-carrying Marxist [who] abolished the House Un-American Activities Committee in the early 1970s, one of the last lines of internal defense. Then you had Frank Church, a very left-wing senator from Idaho, who held his Church Commission in the seventies, which basically hauled our intelligence agencies over the coals.*
>
> *Now, I'm not saying there was no wrongdoing that gave them an opportunity to do this. But Frank Church had served in*

China during World War II with the U.S. military, which is often a sign of Communist sympathies at the time. And he basically destroyed the FBI's willingness to investigate internal subversion in this country and really, really crippled the Central Intelligence Agency.

The CCP's elite capture is not confined to the political world. As Peter Schweizer notes[41]:

If you get a capture in Wall Street, it's kind of a two-fer because, on the one hand, you get the flow of Western capital into China, which is enormously beneficial to their growth and to their military buildup. But you also now capture an institution in America that happens to incorporate probably the largest single group of campaign donors in American politics. So, if you capture Wall Street in a favorable way, you benefit multiple times.

I think that the great irony here is that going back, it really began, I would say, in the early nineties, this notion that engagement with China was going to liberalize them, that it was going to make them be more like us has really backfired. I mean, you see a lot of elites in Wall Street that have actually become more like Beijing than Beijing has become like them. So, you've seen this sort of seismic move by Wall Street elites in sort of favoring the Beijing model of governance. Look, representative government like we have, like it exists in Europe, is messy and it's difficult to deal with if you're a Wall Street titan and you don't have deep principles, you like efficiency.

It is difficult to exaggerate the importance of the insidiousness of China's "Old Friends" on Wall Street serving as lobbyists on China's behalf. Thanks to principals of companies like BlackRock, State Street, Vanguard, and Sequoia, legislation deemed to be a threat to Beijing is routinely neutered, delayed and/or blocked outright. That is especially true of bills that threaten the CCP's access to the trillions of dollars of mostly unwitting American investors, including the pension funds of legislators themselves and other civilian and military federal employees.

The cumulative effect of the elite capture of President Biden, his administration and the leadership of Congress is what can only be described as a "wrecking operation"—a blizzard of executive orders, legislative initiatives, regulations and other policies that have two common denominators: 1) They are all bad for America. And 2) they all benefit—indirectly, if not directly—the Chinese Communist Party and its agenda of destroying this country.

If our constitutional Republic and the liberties it guarantees are to survive, those elite-captured by the Chinese Communist Party must be removed from positions of responsibility and subject, as appropriate, to criminal prosecution. Under no circumstances—and especially not in an environment where actual military conflict is a distinct possibility—can the United States have in its leadership those working for the enemy.

Best-selling author and essayist Lee Smith[42] puts what is required in the starkest terms:

> *The American elite is so corrupt now that the ethics of American elites and the CCP have intersected. What is primarily important to them is their own interests. And the CCP appreciates that. They've built up an enormous internal lobby, so that in order to defend its own interests, [the American elite] will by definition have to protect the CCP. That's really the core issue at stake here. It's not how we break them off from the CCP. Rather it's how we decouple our constitutional republic from that ruling class.*

Charge 4:
The CCP Has Waged Biological Warfare against America and the Rest of the World

Largely unnoted in the list of techniques cited by the two PLA colonels who authored *Unrestricted Warfare* is the recommended use of biological warfare. And that is precisely what the Chinese Communist Party did towards the end of 2019 with a biological attack against the United States and the rest of the world that came to be known as the COVID pandemic.

Before we discuss the evidence to support that statement—and the ways in which the damage wrought worldwide, but especially here, by the Wuhan corona virus was maximized, some context provided by strategic analyst and author J.R. Nyquist[43] is in order:

> *It's important to understand China as a totalitarian country shares the interest in weapons of mass destruction that all totalitarian countries have. They almost have an obsession with [them]. You look at North Korea, for example, you look at Russia under Stalin getting the bomb, getting bioweapons, any kind of weapon of mass destruction. These people are into it. And anybody is naive to think that these are peace-loving governments. They're not.*

> *And this is the challenge, the overall context in which we have to view this [pandemic]: …During the Cold War in 1955, the U.S. military determined that America's food and medicines were vulnerable to biological and toxic attack from enemies abroad. And the Eisenhower administration refused to address the problem then. So, refusing to address this problem is not anything new. A decade later, some military officials approached the government and said, "Look, we do need to get serious about this." Again, the government didn't want to hear it.*

> *In 1969, President Nixon further exacerbated the problem because he eliminated our offensive bio-war program. Why*

that was a problem is that, from that point forward, the only way that the United States would respond to a biological attack is with nuclear retaliation—which is by no means a realistic approach. And we can see why today with the current problem, in 2020, a Chinese virus with very unusual characteristics appeared in Wuhan, China.

We have to now admit that the United States was not prepared for what happened in 2020. And any intentional attack by China, we [also] have to admit, would involve an alibi where the Chinese would have themselves be infected. Well, with a population of 1.4 billion and with a virus that mainly affects the elderly and the infirm, the Communists don't care about that. That's fewer people that their system has to support.

So, you have this pandemic, and you can't determine whether it's an intentional attack. It's very ambiguous. And so, what is the response? How can the United States retaliate with nuclear weapons? It's absurd. And simply put, nobody in authority even wanted to seriously investigate because, if they found something they didn't want to find, that would obligate them to do what exactly? And governments don't like to admit that they're helpless. So even worse, the U.S. government has not even learned a single lesson from the pandemic. It's no exaggeration. to say that our institutions have failed and continue to fail to address the problem of our vulnerability to biological attack, and especially biological attack from China.

A prime example of that failure was evident in an intelligence assessment of the origins of the "COVID-19" virus issued by Director of National Intelligence Avril Haines in October 2021.[44] It was unable to render a judgment as to whether that virus was a naturally occurring phenomenon or the product of laboratory research.

In June of 2022, a blue-ribbon group dubbed Team B III sponsored by the Center for Security Policy and its Committee on the Present Danger: China produced a "second opinion" on the Biden Intelligence Community's seriously deficient assessment in a report entitled, *The CCP is at War with America: The Chinese Communist Party's COVID-19*

Biological Warfare Attack and What's Next.[45] Its key conclusions included the following:

> *[There is] no evidence to support one of the two possible explanations the Director of National Intelligence's assessment offered for the SARS-CoV-2 virus, namely that it was the result of a natural outbreak of an emerging infectious disease. There is, by contrast, a significant body of evidence that indicates the virus was a product of a Chinese laboratory associated with the CCP's illegal biological warfare program: the Wuhan Institute of Virology in Wuhan, China, ground-zero of the initial outbreak.*

> *Such evidence is necessarily, at the moment, circumstantial in nature....[But], the Chinese Communist Party has an active biological warfare (BW) program drawing upon extensive dual-use biomedical research. Open-source writings by senior members of the People's Liberation Army (PLA) have consistently promoted the aggressive pursuit of dual-use genetic biotechnology for future warfare.*

> *It is now known that during the period of 2018-2020 (well before the onset of the COVID-19 pandemic), a series of "gain-of function" genetic experiments were conducted on the spike protein of the coronavirus family. This was a cooperative effort between a U.S. university laboratory and the Chinese Wuhan Institute of Virology. These studies were partially funded by the U.S. National Institutes of Health (NIH), subjected to a moratorium, and then reinstated without proper NIH panel review or NIH supervision.*

> *Following its admission of a new coronavirus outbreak in Wuhan on New Year's Eve 2019, the CCP stated the virus was poorly transmitted from person-to-person and was not a pandemic risk. Yet the Party locked down several of its major cities and prohibited intercity travel to stop viral transmission.*

> *At the same time, the CCP allowed the unrestrained travel of millions of its citizens to international destinations. It also*

attempted to buy up the global supply of individual personal protective equipment for infection control inside China.

The case for concluding that the SARS-CoV-2 virus was a biological weapon that—however it emanated from the Wuhan Institute of Virology—once unleashed in China, was deliberately spread by the Chinese Communist Party to the United States and other parts of the world is further reinforced by other key elements of the Team B III analysis [including the conclusion that] the Chinese have already given us a taste of what appears to be their preferred means of decisively defeating—and, indeed, destroying—the United States: biological warfare. (Emphasis in the original.)

Team B III's Co-Chairman, former Chairman of the House Intelligence Committee Pete Hoekstra[46], expressed deep concern about the official narrative concerning the origins of the SARS-CoV-2 virus:

It's actually frightening to think about the malfeasance of this analysis by the intelligence community, an organization [that] has 18 different branches and spends $70-80 billion per year....It's time to recognize that the Chinese Communist Party is at war with America....China has as its ambition to be the premier, the preeminent global power and [among] the weapons that it has been working on to develop over the last 20 to 30 years, are bio weapons. It may be their preferred way to attack their adversaries in the future.

We believe that it's pretty consistent with the information that is out there that this virus was developed and manipulated in the Wuhan lab. What we do know is what happened once it got outside of the lab: China facilitated the spread of this virus to create a global pandemic and, as the pandemic started to develop early in this process, China destroyed information. It went and cleaned out the Wuhan lab. It deleted all types of scientific information that would have been helpful not only in determining the origins, but also, perhaps how we should respond....Once it got out, they wanted to make sure that the global community would pay a price with this pandemic. They facilitated the travel of millions of Chinese around the world as they locked down Wuhan…and stopped all domestic travel.

Another member of Team B III is Dr. Steven Hatfill, MD, MSc, MSc, M. Med, one of the nation's preeminent scientific experts on biological agents and warfare. He was advising the White House on the COVID virus as the danger posed by the Chinese biological warfare attack first became discernable, then was compounded by the decision to adopt what the CCP calls the "China Model" in response to the pandemic. He described what happens as follows[47]:

> *We know as far back as 2007 that China was conducting what is called gain-of-function experiments. This is taking a pathogen and making it either more infectious or more lethal to man.…*

> *This virus, SARS-CoV-2, appeared out of nowhere, fully adapted to replicate to a high level in human beings.…At the same time [the Chinese] were instructing the World Health Organization to declare that this was not readily person-to-person transmissible…*

> *It was intentional. They knew from a very early stage that it was highly infectious and highly transferable between people. This is why they locked several of their cities down and prohibited inter-city travel. At the same time, they encouraged their population to travel internationally…with the resulting tremendous loss of life.…Technically they were exporting a biological weapon to the population in the United States.*

> *And this can be considered an asymmetrical biological warfare attack. Since that time, there's been nothing but obstruction for Western investigators trying to determine the actual origin [of the virus]. The [established U.S. government pandemic response protocol] was for early drug treatment and we had early drugs that were safe and effective at stopping community spread. But [that protocol] was ignored in favor of experimental new vaccines, which is a different story. But the concept of lockdowns were spread by the Chinese Communist Party to the Western nations. They don't work.*

Dr. Robert Malone, MD, is another top medical practitioner who was troubled by China's role in not only perpetrating the pandemic, but foisting responses that were, at best, ineffective and, at worst, counterproductive and even dangerous. He invented the mRNA technologies recklessly applied in the COVID-19 gene therapies inaccurately described as "vaccines." Dr. Malone observes that[48]:

> We have the strange situation where pre-existing plans and policies that have been documented, developed and intended to be deployed in the event of a major pandemic event…were largely thrown out the door and were substituted or replaced by a set of policies which were actively promoted through various propaganda vehicles by the [Chinese] Communist Party in China.
>
> We have this odd situation where a small group of individuals empowered as Vice President Pence's special committee for managing the COVID crisis…accepted the logic that was being promoted by the [Chinese] Communist Party through a series of what we now know were propaganda actions, including the interjection of images and apparent processes such as: the rigorous authoritarian mass lockdowns; the use of masks; the images of individuals dying and lying on the streets; [uncovered] mass graves and extremely rapid build out of hospitals—all of which were propaganda.
>
> We now know the model that the [Chinese] Communist Party was attempting to advocate for the West—and the West employed based on the idea that this was the model that was being successfully deployed in China—was all propaganda.

The Chinese Communists complemented their own propaganda aimed at encouraging the adoption of a disastrous China Model for responding to the COVID pandemic with support they secured from several dubious sources.

Communists for Lockdowns:

For example, anti-Communist freedom-fighter Trevor Loudon notes[49]:

> *When COVID first really became prominent, the Chinese Communist Party issued a letter signed by 230 worldwide Communist parties, and they had four main points: First, the COVID is not China's fault. Second…the world should be grateful to China for its leadership on combatting COVID. Third, the socialist health system of China has proven way, way superior to the non- socialist health care system of America in combating COVID. And the fourth one was that basically we should be working with China to basically follow China's lead.*

The World Health Organization:

Another key influencer in getting the United States and other nations to adopt the totalitarian China Model was the World Health Organization (WHO). As Dr. Hatfill puts it[50]:

> *The influence of China over the WHO was unrecognized until this pandemic. As a result of China's actions, the WHO refused to provide a timely warning on the human transmissibility of the virus, although it was evident.…The director of the WHO refused to discuss human transmissibility…[and] allowed China to talk him out of declaring a public health emergency.…They also failed to recognize the airborne transmission of the virus as a major route of spread. This is inexcusable.*

> *And most grievously, they endorsed lockdowns and face masks as effective. The data we have now shows that lockdowns did really nothing, maybe drop the death rate by 2%. But basically, at the destruction of any country's economy that followed this policy, long lockdowns. It also promoted face masks as being effective and we know that face masks do very little, especially if your eyes aren't covered.*

> *The WHO fail[ed] to keep up with the concept of early use treatment and the overwhelming evidence of the effectiveness of hydroxychloroquine, and then later on in the epidemic, ivermectin—in spite of the fact that countries like India and Brazil were using these drugs with highly, highly successful results. The WHO was more concerned about changing the*

name from the Wuhan Virus to SARS-CoV-2 because the Chinese didn't like the name....The influence China has had on the WHO has severely compromised this organization's integrity.

The World Health Organization's appalling record in dealing with the COVID pandemic—especially its subordination under Tedros Ghebreyesus to the direction of the Chinese Communist Party—should utterly preclude any consideration of strengthening the power of its Director General to declare Public Health Emergencies of International Concern, let alone impose on sovereign states how they, their public health authorities and people must respond.

Dr. David Bell, M.D., a former senior WHO official, described the increased—and ominous—additional authorities being sought by that organization and its leader as follows:

These amendments greatly expand the definition of health emergencies, including a sort of "One Health" definition which really includes anything that could potentially impact wellbeing or health. And it includes potential threats, rather than real threats. And there's a bureaucracy, a bureaucracy of surveillance that's being set up....The Director-General (DG) of WHO...will have sole power to declare an emergency and to stop an emergency later.

And the other important thing is that the amendments in their current form change recommendation to be binding. So, when countries sign this, if the wording is not changed, they will be signing up to a binding agreement to do what the WHO [says] in any health threat.

Another important aspect of this is the way it addresses human rights....The original language of the international health regulations from 20 years ago or so, includes very similar language to the Universal Declaration of Human Rights after the Second World War. This is being changed to equity coherence and inclusivity, which are really meaningless terms. And importantly, it also is basing these on the social and economic context. So this is taking the whole basis of individual sovereignty, sovereignty and all people equal and turning this into all people are not equal. [Instead] someone who decides based on economic and social assessment of that person will decide what rights they have. And these rights are very, very powerful.

The [amendments to the] international health regulations at the moment include recommendations from the WHO and the DG to do things like closing borders, forced quarantine, confinement of individuals, forced medical examinations, requiring injection, etcetera. But in changing these from recommendations to a binding agreement, what this means is that WHO can tell a person in the United States or Malawi or Vietnam to be injected with a vaccine, for instance, or to have a medical examination or to be confined at home. And rather than having someone even in a country to do this or in a local community, assessing public health risks, this is someone in a completely different part of the world giving broad orders on how people should be treated. So this is completely undoing the whole idea of individual sovereignty and community-based care that WHO was based on.[51]

Efforts by the Biden administration, the CCP and other governments stealthily to foist such a sinister, unaccountable, dangerous and sovereignty-destroying arrangement on the United States of America must be thwarted at all costs.[52]

World Economic Forum:

Yet another source of pressure to conform to China's lockdowns and other freedom-crushing responses to the pandemic was the globalist World Economic Forum and its prime-movers like Bill Gates. As author John Leake observes[53]:

These massive international foundations like the Rockefeller Foundation, Bill and Melinda Gates Foundation working closely with the World Economic Forum have really done a stunning job of, in effect, hijacking international public health policy. This interest in the China Model perhaps should be best understood as something more anthropological in nature than ideological. In the year 2010, the Rockefeller Foundation, in cooperation with the Global Business Network, chaired by a guy named Peter Schwartz, came up with a published set of scenarios looking forward to the 21st Century.

One of the scenarios published in this Rockefeller Foundation document was called "Lock Step" about an emerging epidemic disease that would emanate from China. In the opening paragraphs, a great admiration is expressed for China's response to the emerging disease epidemic—the lockdowns, the masking, the mass quarantines of entire cities. So, we see the Rockefeller Foundation already in 2010 expressing admiration for this sort of response to a global disaster.

The strong connection between the World Economic Forum and the Chinese Communist Party is not generally recognized. As Dr. Malone points out, however[54]:

What's often overlooked is that the World Economic Forum does not just meet in Davos. They also meet annually in China. The World Economic Forum is very much involved in Chinese operations and politics. Larry Fink and BlackRock have over $2 trillion of investment in China....These corporations are now transnational and very, very much integrated into the business model and politics of the CCP.

Particularly troubling is the shared interest the Chinese Communists and Klaus Schwab's World Economic Forum have in weaponizing the pandemic. Dr. Malone says, "What we've observed over the last three years of the COVID crisis has been a great test example of how these technologies of digital passports, digital ID, central bank digital currency-controlled currency, virtual currency can be used as instruments of control and instruments of censorship."

How far along are these technologies? The Executive Secretary of the Committee on the Present Danger: China, Dede Laugesen, reports on the collaborative efforts of the Chinese Communist-dominated WHO and the World Economic Forum to bring them bear in the near future[55]:

> *The World Health Organization announced at the World Health Assembly, hosted in Geneva [in May, 2022] a contract with Deutsche Telecom for the development of a global vaccine passport platform. Meanwhile, at the World Economic Forum's gathering in Davos, Switzerland, radical environmentalists announced plans for a digital carbon footprint tracker to monitor every bite of food, ounce of trash and miles traveled by every citizen of the world. This is massive centralized data collection on an unprecedented scale and a threat to the freedom and privacy of every person everywhere.*

Another point of convergence between the Chinese Communist Party and the World Economic Forum is their common interest in ending the so-called liberal rules-based order created by and associated with the post-World War II United States. They may have different notions as to what will come in its stead—the Middle Kingdom or the Great Reset. But they agree (as do, by the way, Sharia-supremacists) that America must be eliminated as an impediment to the realization of their respective preferred end-states.

A man who has studied closely the devastation of this country wrought by the COVID pandemic and the adoption of the China Model in response to it is Team B III member Kevin Freeman, CFA, an author and television host who is one of America's foremost experts on economic warfare. His findings include the following[56]:

> *What was unleashed by the CCP was biological warfare and perhaps the greatest economic weapon of history. It put America another $8 trillion or so in debt as we went from about $22-and-a-half-trillion to $30-and-a-half-trillion in debt. It brought inflation, caused problems in the stock market, shut down small business. It is the most impactful economic weapon that you can imagine.*
>
> *In the midpoint of Donald Trump's presidency, the economy was strong. We were holding China accountable. Small business was growing. And when this virus was unleashed, it reversed all those favorable American trends and literally traded places and gave China the stronger position.*

They've been a bad actor under any circumstances and we have the bioweapons labs through the NIH and we have funded them with our spending and buying all these Chinese products; moving our plants to China, and worst perhaps of all is we funded them with our stock market investments, including taking money from the pensions of servicemen and women and trying to put them into Chinese stocks.

Women's Rights Without Frontiers founder and President Reggie Littlejohn, an internationally renowned human rights activist and litigator-turned-freedom-fighter, provided a powerful bottom line to the case supporting Charge 4.[57]

In 2019 to 2020, China attacked the world. And regardless of whether the virus was leaked from a lab or whether it came from an animal, what is indisputable is that the Chinese Communist Party deliberately infected the world....They are responsible for every death and all the destruction that has happened as a result of this CCP virus.

With the deeply compromised World Health Organization at the helm, most of the Western world adopted the China model for handling this pandemic...lockdowns, face masks, quarantines, mandatory vaccinations, and all of this tracked by a vaccine passport or digital ID, "Excelsior Pass."

In my opinion, the CCP virus pandemic was a trial run to get the infrastructure in place to institute totalitarian control in the next pandemic....The Chinese Communist Party gives rights—or takes them away. Now, in America, under the state of a health emergency, our own government has taken away substantial rights with vaccine mandates and passports. We can only get them back if we cooperate.

This is a shift to the Chinese Communist Party way of thinking that people do not have God- given rights, but rather our rights are given or taken away by the government. We live in the domain of the state and we only have rights if we are compliant with the government.

The cumulative effect of what was, at a minimum, a Chinese proof-of-concept for a larger and more deadly biological warfare attack has been greatly to compound other aspects of the CCP's unrestricted warfare against the United States discussed in subsequent Charges below. For the present purpose suffice it to say: The combined impact of the Wuhan Virus and the China Model can be characterized as contributing materially to, among other repercussions, hugely advancing the following Chinese Communist priorities vis a vis America's take-down by:

- Profoundly and on a continuing basis damaging the U.S. economy;

- Wantonly increasing federal spending, precipitating vast increases in the national debt and undermining the reserve status of the dollar;

- Generating intense societal dislocation, upheaval and alienation;

- Discrediting and otherwise eroding confidence in government, especially public health officials, and institutions more generally;

- Providing the pretext for universal mail-in voting and other fraud-conducive techniques that have a) prevented free and fair elections in 2020—resulting in the defeat of the CCP's greatest nemesis, President Donald Trump—and in the 2022 mid-terms and b) severely diminished trust in future balloting; and

- Subjecting our constitutionally guaranteed freedoms to myriad restrictions including the introduction of vaccine passports that can and will serve as the infrastructure for the insinuating here the Chinese "social credit system" and the greatest enabler of the "Digital Gulag" it entails: a Central Bank Digital Currency (CBDC).

The end of Xi Jinping's brutally repressive domestic Zero-Covid strategy[58], which massively and at huge cost suppressed herd immunity in China, has raised fears of new strains of the Wuhan virus. At the same time, Xi is reverting to form—opening the floodgates for individuals likely to have been exposed to one variant or another of the disease to travel internationally, including here.

Thanks to President Biden's opening of our southern border, notwithstanding his new-found willingness to impose travel restrictions at *legal U.S. entry points* on those coming from China, there is a high probability that several things will happen as a result of the latest, severe viral outbreak in China: 1) It will result in fresh waves of COVID-related illness, health care crises and deaths. 2) The World Health Organization—which has, as noted above, been busily working with the Biden administration and others to secure ominous new authorities at the expense of member nations' sovereignty[59] over public health policy and practices—will renew its mandate for China Model-style restrictions. And 3) federal and at least *some* state authorities will insist that America must conform once again to WHO guidance.

It is, at this point, anyone's guess as to how the American people will respond to the prospect of being once again told to stay home, mask up, remote school and get jabbed. One certitude is that, if some significant portion of the population refuses to comply with one or more of these edicts, there could be violence. And, if that happens, a principal beneficiary would surely be the Chinese Communist Party.

CHARGE 5:
The CCP Is Taking Down Our Economy and Society—and We Are Paying for It

Since at least the adoption by Deng Xiaoping of the Hide and Bide strategy, the Chinese Communists have had as a centerpiece of their efforts aimed at overtaking and supplanting the United States as the world's dominant power, the destruction of America's industrial base and economic competitiveness. As we discussed in Charge 3, this process has been greatly facilitated by the practice of elite capture, of which a prime target has been U.S. business leaders and the government officials susceptible to their lobbying, influence and campaign donations.

Peter Schweizer, author of *Red-Handed: How America's Elites Get Rich Helping China Win*[60] makes clear the priority assigned by the CCP to suborning the most important people in our economy[61]:

> *I always wondered why the United States is not taking a more proactive position in countering [China]. And what I realized is [the Chinese] have this strategy. They write about it openly of "elite capture." And it's brilliant if you think about it: "Rather than go head-to-head with the United States, we're going to just basically buy off elements of its leadership class, both political parties, people on Wall Street, people in Silicon Valley, people in Washington, D.C. And we're going to effectively decapitate their leadership by doing so." So that is elite capture.*

Capturing the U.S. Financial Sector

Arguably, the single most important facet of this line of attack in the CCP's unrestricted warfare against America has been Beijing's success in inducing the "Old Friends" it has cultivated on Wall Street to divert, by some estimates, between $3-6 trillion dollars from U.S. investors' pension funds, 401(k) plans, mutual funds, exchange traded funds and other investment vehicles to companies in China, *all* of which are either state-owned or controlled by the Chinese Communist Party.

Peter Schweizer addresses this strategic insanity in a very personal way—as he believes *every American investor* should do[62]:

> *About five or six months ago, I looked at my 401(k) investment account as small as it is, and I thought, "Well, I'm not investing in Chinese companies." I [didn't] know. Individual stocks I looked at [included] a Fidelity Developing World emerging global markets fund. 35 to 40% of the companies in that fund were Chinese companies.*
>
> *So, what I would say to the audience out there: Do a serious assessment. If you are invested in an emerging markets fund or a world fund, the odds are overwhelming that you own parts of Chinese companies. And these Chinese companies are not making potato chips. They are making computer chips and they are making components for weapon systems that are aimed at us. So, everybody has to check it. I checked it and was shocked at what I found.*

It is no exaggeration to say that this underwriting of our mortal enemy has greatly facilitated every other aspect of its myriad efforts to take down the United States and otherwise dominate the planet. In fact, whenever one hears credit being given to the CCP for its "economic miracle" of lifting much of its population out of poverty and transforming China into a superpower, it would not have happened without the immense, and essentially unrestricted, capital inflows from American investors whose funds—mostly unbeknownst to them—have been transferred by Wall Street's "masters of the universe."

Incredibly, even as the prospects grow for a shooting war with the Chinese Communist Party U.S. investment managers like Larry Fink's BlackRock, Ray Dalio's Bridgewater, Steve Schwarzman's Blackstone Group, Neil Shen's Sequoia Capital China and others running huge companies, including State Street, Vanguard and Fidelity, remain determined to plow *still more* of Americans' money into Chinese companies controlled by the CCP.

This insistence is lubricated by the same thing that drives the capture of other U.S. elites: Wall Street's mavens have grown enormously rich as they have enabled the CCP's growing menace. So, they choose to ignore the peril for their clients evident in such inconvenient facts as: some $1 trillion in losses sustained in Beijing's tech sector in 2022[63]; the collapse of the Chinese real estate market[64]; China's banking bubble[65]; Xi Jinping's protracted "Zero-COVID" lockdowns; and his capricious interference in PRC securities markets[66]. Even the prospect of violent conflict with China—that would surely result in *the loss of all U.S. investments there*—has yet to translate into Wall Street reducing our exposure to such huge, albeit undeclared, material risk.

Economic warfare specialist Kevin Freeman, CFA, characterizes the magnitude of this risk as follows:

> *When you place investments in China, you're putting them potentially in an undisclosed risk position. We really need to understand that there's undisclosed material risk when you invest in a mutual fund or an ETF or directly in Chinese funds, that it may be something that we have to cut off if we go to war with them. It may be something where they're appropriating our money and using it to build missiles that are aimed at our troops or aimed at us individually....These are serious risks that aren't disclosed.[67]*

Especially egregious has been the efforts made by BlackRock and State Street to invest the pension savings of U.S. military and civilian government personnel in China.[68] As former Reagan Senior NSC Director for International Economic Affairs Roger Robinson recounts, in 2020, President Donald Trump learned and was horrified at: "the notion of having six or seven million federal employees and our uniformed military being in a position where they're either compelled to invest, to the extent that they have international exposure in their portfolios, or even the option to invest in various funds that are inclusive of Chinese bad actor companies, including...[U.S.] sanctioned [ones]."

Mr. Trump ordered a halt to that initiative.[69] But Wall Street did an end-run on his directive.[70] Mr. Robinson describes it this way[71]:

> *This is a very troubling development....Where we sit today is a kind of effort to replay that drama of two years ago. We have found in our research that 35 [Hong Kong-headquartered] Chinese companies have been inserted into the international*

fund of the Thrift Savings Plan, despite the presidential directive contravening…and/or opposing strongly such a step. And we thought it was resolved, but little did we know, it was not.

And now there's an effort to structure what's called a Mutual Fund Window initiative. This [involves] 5000 mutual funds that would be available for up to 25% of the savings of Thrift Savings Plan participants [able and willing to make] a $10,000 buy-in.

If we think about what the CCP has gotten done over these 25 years or so, trillions of dollars…of investment funds from average American retail investors have flowed to the coffers of the CCP. That's trillions with a "t."

A patriotic American financial leader, Kyle Bass, believes that we have not only thus enabled the CCP to become a massive threat. He contends that, unlike many of their financial advisors, U.A. investors whose funds have been used for this purpose have generally not benefited from these transactions[72]:

…If you invested back in December of 1992 in the Chinese indices that were added to the MSCI [index], do you know where you are today, 30 plus years later? You've lost 15% of your money on a price basis. On a total return basis, you've made about 25% to 29%. But that's because they've paid almost 60% in dividends over a 30-year period.

What you're doing is you're giving the Chinese Communist Party your money and they're making [money] and you're making nothing.

[Moreover,] I don't know how you discount genocide risk. I don't know how you discount Xi Jinping, whimsically kneecapping for-profit education…or whatever else he's going to do for the "common prosperity of China."

It's the superhighway of fees that the billionaires are focused on. And again, I've said this many times: If U.S. national security was left to the private sector, Wall Street and the billionaires, we will all be speaking Chinese tomorrow.

...So, we need leadership and we need to understand that we are funding our enemy. Think about what we did. The U.S. funded Germany going into World War II because we were embarrassed about destroying them in World War I. We lent them billions of dollars to build their war machine. We have continued to build Putin's war machine today. And we are absolutely building China's war machine against us in the future.

Exploiting Trade Relations

With help from Wall Street's lobbyists and other business elites, and cash contributions to Bill Clinton's reelection campaign,[73] China secured entry into the World Trade Organization (WTO) in 2000.[74] It has, ever since, selectively adhered to the trade policies mandated by the WTO that advantage Chinese efforts to penetrate and subvert the U.S. economy. It has simultaneously ignored those WTO rules that require the PRC to open up, prevent dumping or otherwise establish reciprocal practices to China's *dis*advantage.[75]

The Chinese Communists have relentlessly exploited such found money and their mutation of the WTO rules, among other things, to perpetrate the following acts of war against the U.S. economy:

Hollowing out the American industrial base

The CCP has followed a basic formula: 1) Get access to U.S. technology and industrial and other economic sectors with the promise of opening up its own vast markets to investment and consumer sales. 2) Exploit such access, state subsidies, intellectual property acquisition (legal and illegal) and techniques like dumping to secure dominant positions in American markets and bankrupt China's competition here and elsewhere around the world. 3) Create strategic supply chain dependencies on China that can be constricted or cut off at the direction of the CCP.

Nathan Carson, vice president of Operations at Chemical Dynamics, Inc. describes the allure in the nineties of China's markets and cheap labor force[76]:

China was able to exploit this because, back in the nineties, it had...over a quarter of all the world's manpower in terms of being able for the workforce. It's something like 735 million workers in China that it was able to bring to bear, all this mass cheap labor. And so, all of these big corporations were vulnerable and were foaming at the mouth, wanting to get a hold of this market, these cheap goods with globalization and make more money. And the CCP has exploited that. They've particularly targeted the transfer of critical industries such as agriculture, with gene-editing technology.

Rosemary Gibson co-authored *China Rx: Exposing the Risk of America's Dependence on China for Medicine*,[77] a detailed study of the CCP's systematic take-down of U.S. manufacturers of such indispensable therapies as aspirin, penicillin, Vitamin C and most of the ingredients of generic and other life-saving prescription medications. The book documents, as she put it, that[78]:

Large [U.S.] companies gave away their recipes, their formulations for medicines, to the Chinese in return for access to the Chinese market for their more lucrative branded products. And that's how we got here. And that is why we see, I believe, opposition to domestic manufacturing of things that we need to survive.

The blight known as "the Rust Belt" in America's heartland is a direct result and enduring symptom of such unrestricted economic warfare by China. Nathan Carson is an executive in the fertilizer industry who has closely studied how the Chinese took full advantage of a proclivity baked into free enterprise—profit-making—to promote globalization and its most predictable and dangerous by-product: supply chain dependencies on what has been for decades the lowest-cost manufacturing nation, namely, the PRC[79].

My family owns a small business. My grandfather started the company almost 50 years ago... And so [I] understand that [the] entrepreneurial spirit and desire to better oneself is part of the American dream. It's part of our free market capitalist system. But where we went wrong is with the libertarian mindset that the most moral thing that a company can do is make a profit.

It was this idea that greed is good and that the highest order good for political economy is wealth maximization that… resulted in this just unfettered exploitation of globalization. It's what's turned the arsenal of democracy into the Rust Belt. And that mindset over the past 50-60 years has infiltrated not just corporate America, it's infiltrated big law, it's infiltrated our university system. It's infiltrated every aspect of government, which is why we saw under the Obama administration, not just the approval of Smithfield Foods being bought out by the Chinese[80], but also Syngenta [a key seed and pesticide manufacturer] being bought out by the Chinese.[81]

…A lot of the players in the Obama administration that were in those key positions are in key positions under the Biden administration. So, unfortunately…our government regulators and officials have been asleep at the wheel a while for quite some time.

The acquisition of American farmland and other real estate purchases—including some in proximity to strategic U.S. assets

As but one example of the non-reciprocal nature of Chinese economic warfare against the United States, the CCP has taken advantage of a lax federal oversight process known as the Committee on Foreign Investment in the United States (CFIUS). Run by the Treasury Department, which reflexively favors foreign investment in the United States, CFIUS infrequently blocks such transactions, even when national security considerations warrant their rejection.

In the absence of the needed adult supervision, the PRC been able, among other things, to secure state and local support—and, in some cases, *subsidies*—for Beijing's land purchases in this country on the grounds that they will produce employment and other benefits for the affected communities. "According to the organization Good Jobs First, since 2010 U.S. state and local governments have provided nearly $2 billion in subsidies to Chinese companies investing in the United States."[82]

Economic warfare expert Kevin Freeman notes[83]:

The Chinese have used the elites in America to do this. It's not just Hunter Biden, the laptop, but that's included. It's all of the other politicians that have been bought off since the 1990s, including Charlie Trie, a Little Rock restaurant entrepreneur who was funneling money into the Clinton reelection campaign.[84]

The Chinese have been buying off politicians. They've been buying off businesspeople. They've been buying our companies. They've been buying our farmland.

They're using all of these methodologies, including dumping, proprietary information theft, intellectual property theft, joint ventures, techniques that are de-industrializing America and leading us to supply chain dependencies. If we were on a war-footing, we would address this crisis. [And] we should.

The CCP's penetration of America's agricultural sector has been facilitated by the U.S. Department of Agriculture (USDA). Nathan Carson describes its conduct this way[85]:

USDA has really taken a laissez-faire approach to what's going on. If anything, it has encouraged the export of agricultural commodities to China.

When Trump instigated the trade war against China, China immediately retaliated against U.S. farmers because China understood that farmers were a key constituent of the Trump administration and also...that the industry that was most heavily reliant upon exports to China was the U.S. ag sector.

And the USDA has done a terrible, terrible job of encouraging diversification of exports. And the thing is, in business, you never become reliant upon one customer or one vendor.... If you're an investor, you have to diversify. Your investment portfolio of American agriculture for exports and imports is heavily concentrated on China, and that allows it to pull these asymmetrical levers and engage in irregular war.

And so, the USDA, more than anything, needs to be knocking down doors in Africa, in the Middle East and saying, "You need food right now. We'll send it to you." And start diverting U.S. food from China and start sending it to these other countries, as well as using food as a tool of diplomacy to counteract Russian influence in this region, to counteract the Chinese.

If the Chinese want to play tough, let them try to source their food from somewhere else. If they want to become Best Friends Forever with the Russians, let them try to truck it across and pay the extra fees of trying to bring it across the Siberian wasteland. That's how the United States needs...to play.

In some cases, such Chinese land acquisitions have had clear, adverse national security risks due to their proximity to sensitive military bases, implications for the electric grid, etc. Yet, they have often received scant scrutiny, let alone been blocked. In fact, CFIUS recently declared that land purchases are not within the Committee's purview.[86]

A recent case in Texas illustrates the dangers associated with such a stance. One of the few prominent leaders of the U.S. financial sector who harshly criticizes the Chinese Communist Party is Committee on the Present Danger: China member Kyle Bass. He became engaged in efforts to block a retired Chinese general's acquisition a 200-square mile property and its development as a solar farm in proximity to a sensitive American pilot training facility in south Texas: Laughlin Air Force Base. Thanks to Mr. Bass' personal intervention with the Texas legislature, the general's wind farm will not be allowed to tie into the state's electric grid.[87] Yet, the former PLA officer's ownership and development of the vast purchase continues.

Mr. Bass recently flew over the land in question and found that[88]:

...This Chinese general is ploughing more capital into building a runway, into building multiple facilities along the runway, into building a lodge, into building guest facilities for their charm offensives with local politicians. This has got to stop. What we need to do to address this issue, not only in the state of Texas, but in the U.S. writ large, is change the way the laws of the CFIUS works.

...Today, the way those laws are put into place and executed are an acquisition of that type of property, which is proximate to military bases or sensitive, critical infrastructure, gets a review by CFIUS. And once it passes a review, the triggering mechanisms for a re-review are additional property acquisitions as part and parcel of that ownership stake or a change in specific use of the property that was different than what was submitted to CFIUS in the first place. Now, the Chinese are smart and the malign state actors other than China are smart. They know not to trip an additional CFIUS review.

My view is the CFIUS laws must be changed so that a re-review can happen at any time without a triggering mechanism. And that's what's needed here. It's obvious [that] it's a clear and present danger to our national security. And somehow, some way, this one happened to get through CFIUS.

Another example of a problematic land purchase the CFIUS declined to stop involved a bid by a Chinese conglomerate called Fufeng Group to acquire a corn-milling facility near Grand Forks Air Force Base. Author and historian Scott Powell studied this transaction and found that what Kyle Bass calls "malign state actors" appear to be either ignorant or *willfully* blind to the fact that "the Communist Party was calling the shots on the Fufeng USA corn-milling plant" and that, if the CCP's role were known in the community, the purchase would be "dead in the water." He observes[89]:

...[The deal's proponents in North Dakota] don't talk about that. But you don't have to...be an in-depth scholar of how the CCP works to know that these things are not going to be run independently by some American company [like] Fufeng, USA....You know, they would market it as a completely independent American company that happens to be affiliated with Fufeng in China, but it's going to really be an American provider of jobs. And they pump that up, not ever talking about the political implications [and] the security implications of the CCP [involvement].

Fortunately, as local press reported, the Air Force finally declared on January 30, 2023 that "the proposed project presents a significant threat to national security with both near- and long-term risks of significant impacts to our operations in the area." Those operations reportedly include: "U.S. intelligence, surveillance and reconnaissance units, including its top-secret drone technology." [90, 91]

It is unclear why such concerns were not expressed from the get-go, sparing the community and the country an entirely avoidable public thrash about the dangers associated with this CCP acquisition. With the Air Force assessment in hand, however, the city council of Grand Forks finally voted on February 6, 2023 to block the deal. [92]

Needless to say, the Chinese Communist Party would never tolerate reciprocal purchases of these sorts of properties in the People's Republic by U.S. business interests—let alone any tied to our government and its security agencies. Nathan Carson puts it this way[93]:

> *Because the CCP is a totalitarian government, if you want to do any sort of investing in China, you're going in with at least a 50/50 ownership split. And, at any time, the CCP can come in and confiscate all your assets if you do anything to piss off the ruling government or provincial leader. And a lot of U.S. companies are beginning to realize that. So no, there is absolutely no reciprocity whatsoever.*

Food Hoarding and Other Leading Indicators of the CCP's Adopting a War-Footing

As Nathan Carson notes in the previous section, one area in which the United States has a competitive advantage over Communist China is in food production. With its history of famines—both naturally induced and inflicted by the CCP—the ruling regime in Beijing is keenly mindful that food insecurity can jeopardize its hold on power. It is, therefore, going to considerable lengths to obtain and stockpile food certain to be needed, especially in the event of a kinetic war with America.

Food security expert Ross Kennedy warns about some of the critical foodstuffs and other products being exported in large quantity to the CCP[94]:

> *Exported food from the United States [includes] our raw materials, things like corn, soybeans, eggs or distiller's dried*

grains or soluble, which is a feed ingredient that comes from production of ethanol and the dry corn milling process, or finished product [such as] packaged animal proteins like frozen beef or fish or chicken, frozen pork. Obviously, a Chinese entity owns Smithfield Pork, which is a very famous CFIUS case that in my view, was poorly adjudicated…in 2014.[95]

The Chinese Communist Party is not only buying up large amounts of productive U.S. farmland and exporting its harvests to China. It has also been acquiring a number of this country's food processing plants, at a time when—coincidentally or not—many others are burning down, being struck by planes or otherwise going off-line.

Nathan Carson depicts the dangers associated with the coincidence of these two trends[96]:

We've allowed for the greater concentration of our agri-food systems [which include] about 16 pork producers [that] produce about over 60% of U.S. pork. which means if you knock out a few of those processors, like during the pandemic, man, now you're hurting. You don't have access to the pork that you needed for meat.

And so, the concentration of our industry under the guise of Big Business in the pursuit of profit has made our agrifood supply chains…more fragile. And they're easier to exploit that way. When you decentralize the supply chain, it's more resilient from exogenous shocks, and it's really a lot more difficult for foreign actors like the Communist Chinese to infiltrate these critical nodes.

These actions have been accompanied by China's sustained stockpiling of food at what have been described as "historically high levels." As of a year ago, it had "more than half of the world's maize and other grains" and according to the U.S. Department of Agriculture, China will hold 69% of the world's corn reserves, 60% of its rice, and 51% of its wheat by mid-2022.[97]

The Chinese Communist Party has also sought to *reduce our competitive advantage*—and their supply chain dependency—with regard to U.S. food exports by restricting exports to American farmers of fertilizers and their components. Nathan Carson points out that[98]:

> Today, China makes up about 30% of global manufacturing.[99]
> China actually makes up about 40% of all global chemical
> manufacturing,[100] which means you're looking at chemical
> precursors that go into pharmaceuticals, different industrial
> goods [and] amino acids that different animal proteins need in
> order for these animals, poultry, hogs, cattle, etc., to be able to
> grow, to be healthy. Otherwise, you have just a massive, massive
> problem and you have a collapse of our animal ag systems if you
> don't have these amino acids in very particular detail.
>
> But on the fertilizer side of things, you're looking at things like
> pesticides, the herbicides, the insecticides that you need in order
> to keep your crops going and being healthy. You also have these
> chemical precursors that are coming in for just basic lubricants
> and chemicals just to keep factories running....So, it's a major
> supply chain vulnerability that the United States has. It's been
> exploited by China.

The CCP Builds the Colonial Infrastructure for a Global Empire

Another dimension of the CCP's use of economic instruments to wage unrestricted warfare in furtherance of its bid for global domination is Xi Jinping's Belt and Road Initiative (BRI). As a July 2021 study by the Committee on the Present Danger: China and its Captive Nations Coalition entitled, *China's Dream, The World's Nightmare: How the Chinese Communist Party is Colonizing and Enslaving the Planet,* put it[101]: "The Belt and Road Initiative (BRI) is a massive campaign by the Chinese Communist Party (CCP) to achieve world domination by building an empire through massive debt-trap financed overseas investments and commercial transactions."

CPDC member Steven Mosher is the president of the Population Research Institute and author of a number of important books including, "*Bully of Asia: Why China's Dream Is the New Threat to World Order.*"[102] He observes that[103]:

The Belt and Road Initiative…is nothing less than China's plan to colonize the world….The Belt and Road Initiative is key to China's plan to dominate. It consist[s] of two things: a Silk Road economic belt, the land route, and the maritime Silk Road, the sea route. The land route through Asia is a series of roads, rail lines and shipping terminals across the Eurasian landmass. The Maritime Silk Road, shipping lanes, ports and cargo handling facilities would link China by sea to South Asia, Africa and Europe.

The Belt and Road Initiative has continued to expand over the years. Sixty-one countries joined in 2018. By 2021, 139 countries were formally affiliated. By this year, the number seems to be around 147….It is now global.

The *China's Dream, the World's Nightmare* report explains how the BRI works[104]:

The Belt and Road Initiative is a prime example of imperialism achieved by using China's ability to extend massive loans— thanks in no small measure to financing from U.S and other Western capital markets—to many poverty-stricken and/ or corrupt countries at high-risk of defaulting on such loans. When countries cannot make their loan payments, the PRC takes ownership by various means of the infrastructure thus financed and/or valuable land, natural resources, and even the sovereignty of these distant lands. Thanks to the BRI, China is rapidly extending its territory, power and influence on a truly global scale.

Steve Mosher underscores the value of the BRI to the CCP as it seeks to project and profit from its power globally[105]:

The Belt and Road Initiative…is not merely an economic venture. Nothing undertaken by the Chinese Communist Party is undertaken without first considering the primary concern of the CCP—which is, holding and increasing its political power and control. And so the Belt and Road Initiative, in strategic terms, is a $1 trillion program to secure economic and political *military dominance over all of Europe, Asia and Africa, what Mackinder called "the world island."[106]*

It is also to isolate India, which may be a precursor, a warning for the United States, and how we might one day be isolated. And of course,…that's its end goal. Its penultimate goal is to displace European and American power.

The BRI's infrastructure investments and related projects not only afford the Chinese Communists vehicles for penetrating, influencing, elite-capturing and dominating markets and resources in participating countries. It also creates truly unprecedented opportunities for power-projection in regions all over the world.

Several of those regions are of particular concern:

The Western Hemisphere:

With the fraudulent election of Lula da Silva restoring a full-on Communist to power in Brazil, *every major nation in this hemisphere* is governed by Marxists and/or regimes submissive to Beijing—including Canada and our own country. Thanks to its BRI, elite capture and other influence operations, the Chinese Communist Party is deeply present in and involved with virtually, if not literally, every one of those nations.

Joseph Humire is a leading American national security practitioner with extensive experience in the region and deep knowledge of its penetration by hostile powers. Drawing upon his service as a Marine Corps combat veteran and Executive Director of the Center for a Secure Free Society, he observes that[107]:

Even U.S.-friendly presidents, market-friendly presidents, even [what] you could call center-right presidents in the region viewed China as simply an economic option or partner. And really, [they] were a bit short-sighted on some of the more geopolitical or strategic dimensions of what that could mean.

If we go back 20 years ago, China was really a negligible player in all 12…South American nations. If you fast forward ten years, China became the top trade partner of five of the 12 *sovereign nations in South America by 2010. And then if you fast-forward to 2020, China is now the top trade partner for nine of the 12 sovereign nation states in South America. That is an increase of approximately $180 billion in trade that China did, up from 2000 to 2010 to close to $500 billion that they're doing in trade as of 2020. So, they've increased their economic footprint through trade.*

The House Foreign Affairs Committee issued a report that was updated on October 25, 2022, which found that there are 7 BRI countries in Latin America.[108] Joseph Humire estimates there may be 20 or so that have signed on or are in the process of doing so.

To cite but one manifestation of this ominous development: The CCP owns and/or operates some forty ports in Latin America that obviously will facilitate enormously expanded imports of Chinese manufactured goods and exports of raw materials.[109] But, they are also capable of supporting, among other things, the naval forces of the People's Liberation Army.

Francisco Tudela, a former First Vice President of Peru, warns in particular about what China is doing in this connection in his strategically located country.[110]

If the U.S. loses the western coast of the Pacific, then you have a real menace in your rear [echelon]. China is building a huge port in [Chancay], Peru. [It] is a commercial port, but it's the first port that is being built 100% by China in Latin America.[111] It's a huge port with a very deep capacity that could hold the logistics for Chinese People's Liberation Army Fleet Task Force, and that would counteract in the South Pacific, where the U.S. and Britain are working with Australia to equip Australia with nuclear submarines to face the Chinese menace.

Joseph Humire warns[112]:

The Number One call for the United States at this moment is to start prioritizing Latin America. Latin America is no longer a foreign policy backwater. It's not [America's] backyard. It's not the last page of a national security briefing. It needs to be the Number One, Tier One national security and foreign policy priority for the United States. Because if we don't have a safe, secure and prosperous neighborhood, it's impossible to have a safe, secure and prosperous United States."

The Western Pacific:

The CCP's BRI-branded colonialism, its growing military presence, "Wolf Warrior" diplomacy[113] and outright seizure of atolls claimed by others, but that it has nonetheless converted into heavily armed bastions, have transformed the South China Sea and much of the rest of the Western Pacific into, at best, contested waters. At worst, the airspace, oceans and underseas domains of this vast region are becoming effectively controlled by the Communist Chinese.[114]

The implications of that development for the sovereignty, economies and national security of island and Pacific littoral nations—including many long allied with and nominally under the protection of the United States—are grim. The same is true for our own vital interests, as well.

Retired Marine Colonel Grant Newsham draws on his long experience in uniform, as a foreign service officer and business executive in the Pacific to describe the significance of China's growing "island-hopping" political influence and political warfare operations aimed at the isolated microstates and other nations throughout the Western Pacific[115]:

I would encourage people to consider the entire map, not just the South China Sea, not just the Central Pacific and South Pacific, but go all the way to the west coast of Latin America, where you now have leftist governments in place [including] most of the countries along the [hemisphere's] western edge and the eastern edge, too. And what you have is the potential— and don't think China doesn't understand it—for eventually getting the Chinese military, [its] navy and air force in particular, operating from the west coast of Latin America, and the potential for dominating the entire region.

What you're seeing is actually the political component of an insurgency.... And it's worth considering that an insurgency is always 90% political and 10% fighting or military. And that's the important thing to remember. That's how the Chinese have gone about establishing a presence throughout the entire Pacific region.

It's a predictable sequence. It starts with a commercial presence with Chinese people operating businesses. There are investments from China. And this leads to political influence. It creates a constituency in every island or country that sees China as an attractive option and only last does a military strategy complete the third stage of this sequence. And we're going to see it more and more throughout the region.

Russia:

The so-called "No-Limits Partnership" unveiled by Xi Jinping and Vladimir Putin on 4 February 2022[116] on the margins of the Genocide Games in Beijing seems designed to cement what is actually a strategic alliance between a liege lord and a vassal. It clears the way for intensified exploitation of the resources of Russia by China and sets the stage for mutual support in their respective areas of operations. Increasing collaboration between, transfers of weapons technologies by and joint exercises involving the two countries' forces is an ominous portent of what may be in the offing at their hands.[117]

Strategist, essayist and author J.R. Nyquist, explains that[118]:

In the 1990s, you have this growing collaboration between Russia and China to where you have Chris Cox of the Cox Commission in 1999 testifying before the Senate that Russia had been giving massive support to Chinese missile and nuclear developments.[119] You also had open military liaisons between Russia and China beginning in 1999 with the Kosovo war, when they both had reasons to complain about the West and NATO in Serbia and the remaining Yugoslav state.

And then you had the formation...of the Shanghai Cooperation Organization and a growing number of summits between Russia and China, culminating in Putin's visit to China on February 4th [2022], shortly before he began the war in Ukraine. And you've got the testimony of Mr. Wang...

of Lude Media, saying that a secret military alliance was signed in February between the Russian Federation and China and that China is supporting, in unseen ways, Russia's efforts in Ukraine.[120]

Retired Navy Captain James Fanell formerly served as the Chief of Intelligence for the U.S. Pacific Fleet. He has long warned about the growing operational military relationship between Russia and the People's Republic of China. He observes[121]:

In [the] beginning, the Russians looked down on the Chinese and had kind of derision for them. But over the course of the last 20 years, the Chinese not only were able to build up a modern military force of great capability, but they started to be able to exercise with Russian counterparts across larger and larger swaths of the earth—operating in the East China Sea, operating together in the Mediterranean, and then operating together in the Baltic....We've seen increased alignment between their militaries, the trading of information and cooperation. And, Russia's opinion of the PLA has dramatically changed over the last 20 years. They no longer are derisive of them.

So, you [have] Chinese and Russians working closely together in…naval surface combatant activity. And we're seeing more and more of that as their surface warships are working together in cooperation to bring combined fires against what would be a combined U.S. and Japanese fleet in some kind of defense of Taiwan.

Africa, Asia and Europe:

All three of these regions are being subjected to relentless efforts by Communist China to: suborn and otherwise capture local elites; establish infrastructure beachheads (ports, airfields, railroads, road networks, energy grids, telecommunications systems, etc.) on which the PRC can foreclose when, not *if*, payments are missed on their CCP pay-day loan-financing schemes. The pretext offered by such projects to insert Chinese construction workers and camp-followers, means that many of them will marry and procreate with locals. Thus, it created a permanent colonial presence and an expatriate cadre capable of constituting on Beijing's command a PRC 5th Column in strategic countries.

For example, as detailed in the CPDC's 2021 report, *China's Dream, the World's Nightmare*:

> *South Africa is the Chinese Communist Party's prime partner in Beijing's efforts to penetrate and dominate the African continent through its Belt and Road Initiative, propaganda, mass migration and other techniques. China is South Africa's biggest export market and a major source of investment. For example, the two nations have entered into 93 economic and trade deals worth over $1.7 billion in the past year [2020] alone.*
>
> *As a major player in the Southern African Customs Union, South Africa also helps promote the BRI and other Chinese ventures to African nations with great effect. With South Africa's support, China was involved in structuring the African Continental Free Trade Area (AfCFTA), which came into effect in November 2020.*
>
> *According to BRI analyst Chris Devonshire-Ellis, "The AfCFTA deal…is set to provide a huge boost to Africa-China trade, with some estimates suggesting it will rise by 50% in the next 12 months. That will spur further infrastructure development and increase China's role in Africa exponentially."*

In addition, in early 2023, the South African military hosted naval exercises with the PLA Navy and its Russian counterpart—a portentous strategic development that will surely translate into similar opportunities with other of the continent's nations[122].

Obadiah Mailafiya, a one-time Nigerian presidential candidate who formerly served at the African Development Bank, urged African governments to "read the small print" in their BRI paperwork to avoid Beijing's seizure of assets—something that is, as he notes, happening in Madagascar, Kenya, Zambia and Zimbabwe. He suspects Nigeria has leveraged its oil fields as collateral for BRI loans.

In Europe, as Greece began struggling with a profound financial crisis in 2007, it discovered that Communist China was one of very few countries willing to invest in its troubled economy. In the years since, the Chinese Communist Party has parlayed the opening to Europe thus created into a major strategic penetration of the European Union and the NATO alliance.

Starting in 2016, the Greek government allowed a PRC state-owned enterprise that has been sanctioned by the United States, Chinese Ocean Shipping Company (COSCO), to exercise operational control of the port of Piraeus. It has become the fastest-growing cargo and commercial port in the world, the 4th busiest port in Europe, and the lead port for the Mediterranean. "For Beijing, this Mediterranean trade hub is the showpiece investment for the globe-spanning Belt and Road Initiative. But for Washington and its EU allies, it's a worrisome foothold for Chinese influence in the West," says Eric Reguly of *The Globe and Mail.*[123]

Chinese ambitions are unlikely to be confined to Greece or elsewhere in Europe where the Belt and Road Initiative is already taking hold as the CCP seeks to further its predatory economic plans for linking Asia and Europe. China's long string of port control and investment—whether it is in the Mediterranean, Latin America, the Indian Ocean, South and East Asia or Africa—is a harbinger of China's increasing dominance not only in trade, but militarily, as well.

For instance, Chinese investments in the ports of Djibouti, Sri Lanka and Pakistan have been followed by Chinese naval deployments in each country. The good news is that, while PLA Navy warships have already paid goodwill visits to Greece's Piraeus port, the Chinese have not yet publicly declared their intention to turn European ports into PRC military bases. The bad news is that the presence of Chinese personnel in, let alone their running of, these strategic facilities is, at a minimum, a security threat to Europe's seaports and NATO vessels that use them.

Kazakhstan is Central Asia's largest landmass country sharing its borders with Chinese-occupied East Turkistan and Russia with access to the Caspian Sea. Kazakhstan has become ominously reliant on the PRC to buck up its faltering economy. This dependency has greatly facilitated Xi Jinping's determined bid to transform the country into a vassal state. Already "China controls approximately 20 percent of Kazakhstan's oil production and has constructed one of the world's longest oil pipelines, running 2,300 km from the Caspian Sea to Xinjiang province."[124] The quasi-state debt of Kazakhstan to China has increased in just five years to over $20 billion.

The corrupt Kazakh government allows Chinese authorities to act with impunity, resulting in frequent violations of the human rights of native Kazakhs and Uyghurs, and serial breaches by the CCP of Kazakhstan's environmental regulations and antitrust and labor laws. Disputes with Chinese authorities are resolved by Chinese agents accountable only to the CCP, an affront to Kazakh sovereignty and ominous portent of worse to come.

In short, the Chinese Communist Party has, through its unrestricted warfare's economic leading edge done enormous and intensifying damage to the United States, its people and society—and created conditions elsewhere that conduce to Beijing's ability to prevail in a global kinetic conflict should it deem that necessary to restore China to the status of ruler of "all under heaven."

As China expert Gordon G. Chang reminds us, the Chinese Communist Party under its current emperor, Xi Jinping, is determined to achieve that goal, *literally*[125].

> *The Chinese regime is the most ambitious in history, and we'll start our discussion on July 1st, 2021. And on that day, Xi Jinping, the Chinese ruler, marked the centennial of China's ruling organization. And he, in widely reported remarks, said that he was going to crack skulls and spill blood. But in more ominous language on that day, he also said: "The Communist Party of China and the Chinese people, with their bravery and tenacity, solemnly proclaim to the world that the Chinese people are good at not only taking down the old world, but also good in building a new one."*[126]
>
> *These words mean that Xi is trying to impose China's imperial era system, in which Chinese rulers believe that they not only have the mandate of heaven to rule the PRC or all under heaven, but that also [that] heaven compelled them to do so.*
>
> *Now, many historical figures have wanted to rule the world, but Xi Jinping is probably the first to also want to rule the solar system. In 2018, Chinese officials talked about both the moon*

and Mars as sovereign Chinese territory. This is not just idle chatter because everyone can sense that war is coming in Asia.

Those prospects are further increased by the success the CCP and its friends have enjoyed in three other, critically important lines of attack against America: crushing its energy security; hollowing out the U.S military; and fracturing and subverting our country and its institutions.

Charge 6:
The CCP and Its Allies Have Ravaged America's Energy Security

One of the greatest strengths of the United States in any competition with the Chinese Communist Party—especially in time of war—is America's prodigious capacity to translate vast fossil fuel and other natural resources into domestic energy and national security. That abundance also enhances the economic prosperity and safety of friendly nations through reliable supplies particularly of American oil and natural gas. Their enhanced security helps frustrate the CCP's agenda of separating the U.S. from its allies and enslaving all of us, in turn.

Hence, taking down our energy sector is a high priority for our enemies in Beijing. And they are being greatly aided and abetted by those in this country who—whether in the name of mitigating climate change, improving "equity," encouraging depopulation or some other highly dubious utopian agenda—are undermining our energy security.

Economic warfare expert Kevin Freeman CFA explains the stakes involved in the disruption or degrading, to say nothing of the outright destruction, of America's electric grid and/or our sources of fossil fuel production—steps currently being engineered by the CCP and its enablers here[127]:

> I study economics. And I want to share with you [that] this grid/energy problem and the Chinese Communist Party and how they're attacking it really is an economic problem.... [That's] because the economy requires electricity. There's not a function that we do that doesn't require some form of energy, especially electricity, whether you're in retail, whether you're in manufacturing, whether you're in finance, everything depends on electricity.
>
> Our enemies understand that's a reality that we know. It's not just a risk to life. It's not just a risk to our way of life, which

clearly a grid failure would be….If we don't have water, we die. If we don't have medicines, we die. If we don't have food, we die.

It's also a risk to our economy, a direct impact of risk. And you can see that if you step back for a moment and think about the difference between a First World nation and a Third World nation and how they operate. And you realize, Third World nations generally don't operate as effectively or efficiently. They don't have the economic activity, in part because they don't have a stable electric grid. And without the stability of the electric grid, they can't function as businesses. So, it needs to be reliable. We've seen that in the First World here in Texas.

Longtime senior energy executive Dave Walsh echoes this point and underscores the role the U.S. government itself is playing in eroding our energy security[128]:

We're in very troubled times with the administration's minions through the EPA, Department of the Interior, the SEC and now Treasury, all coming at the same mantra on "Let's eliminate our dependence on fossil fuels," which is irrational and moves the country in a very Third World direction.

The Committee on the Present Danger: China's Chairman, Brian Kennedy, provides[129] an ominous explanation for such self-destructive policies:

… (L)et's first say this whole question about the electrical grid, electric vehicles, the national shift away from fossil fuels has very little to do with the environment and more to do with political controls. And this has really been a theme of the American left, especially in California, for a half century.

…My greatest concern is that this whole push towards de-carbonization is really about control of the population—and its control of the population done in a very CCP-friendly way, given how much they will benefit from this hard push toward electric vehicles. And it bears very little relationship to the reality of the true energy capabilities of the United States.

The following are among the techniques the CCP and its captured elites in this country are employing to penetrate, subvert or otherwise diminish the U.S. energy sector.

'Climate Change' and the Environment, Social, Governance (ESG) Gambit

Communist China and its fellow travelers in the West—notably, assorted "globalists" associated with the World Economic Forum, Wall Street's capital markets, the International Monetary Fund, World Bank and various regional "development banks," "green" activists and Marxists in governments around the world—have seized upon preventing dangerous "climate change" as a pretext for destroying the indispensable engine of enhanced quality of life, prosperity and security: inexpensive energy made possible by the exploitation of fossil fuels.

The so-called "Green New Deal" and similar efforts elsewhere have set in motion the abandoning of "non-renewables" like nuclear power and fossil fuels (i.e., coal, oil and natural gas) as sources of energy in favor of "renewables," principally wind and solar power. Such initiatives have two benefits for the CCP:

First, they deprive the United States, her allies and others of the relatively inexpensive and abundant means of providing for electricity-generation, transportation, manufacturing and other applications vital to national security and economic growth. And second, it makes the world *more* dependent on China for lithium and other rare earth minerals used in batteries, wind turbines and solar panels largely produced, and therefore controlled, by the Chinese Communists.

Insult is added to injury insofar as, at the same time that we are becoming hooked on yet another supply chain they dominate (for example, the International Energy Agency (IEA)[130] found in July 2022 that the Chinese solar industry is absolutely dominant over the international solar supply chain), the PRC is building vast numbers of coal-fired power plants to enhance its own energy security and independence.[131]

As Dave Walsh puts[132] it:

> [The CCP's] internal energy policy is all about self-sufficiency. It is all about their own defense. Excepting for oil, which they

don't have a lot of—[pumping only] about 4.9 million barrels a day domestically, the electricity sector [is] being entirely domesticized for their own defense and their own security. Which you know is common sense 101. That's what one would expect. But this pushing out of renewables from China at very high cost to the West I think is telling as a strategy...of theirs.

The CCP's parallel agendas aimed at simultaneously eroding U.S. energy resilience and enhancing its own have been greatly advanced by those like Larry Fink, the CEO of BlackRock, and other Wall Street mavens who have earned billions doing business with *and for* the Chinese Communist Party.

Fink has of late become notorious for relentlessly pursuing two *mutually incompatible* priorities: 1) promoting "environment, social and governance" (ESG)[133] and 2) massively increasing American investments in a China that is *profoundly hostile* to E, S and G.[134] Fink uses BlackRock's large ownership stakes in many leading American companies and "ESG scoring" like a cudgel to coerce them to embrace his "Woke" agenda of so-called "stakeholder" capitalism, instead of the free-market kind focused first and foremost on return-on-investment for shareholders.

At the same time Fink is upending our energy sector, he has recommended *tripling* investment in Chinese companies, effectively driving ever-more found-money capital to the CCP. Apparently, he is completely indifferent to the fact that, according to Dave Walsh[135], "China is building as we speak, 19 more large coal plants. Last year, coal use [there] elevated [to] 220 million metric tons. This year, 350 metric tons."

The president of Consumers' Research, Will Hild, characterizes the anti-American investment practices of the BlackRock CEO this way[136]:

Larry Fink is doing the bidding of the CCP and his work over there supports that. So, he's funneled billions at this point, probably trillions, of dollars of investment capital into CCP-controlled companies. He doesn't require [of them] any of the same ESG-style platitudes or tributes that he requires of domestic companies here in the United States.

In fact, just to...give you a concrete example, last year, Larry and BlackRock used their 7.5% control of shares of Exxon to help elect three radical environmentalists to the board of that company. The stated goal in their campaign to become board of directors [members] was that Exxon wasn't doing enough in "renewable energy" and [it...was] doing too much in the business of oil and gas recovery.

And so, with the election of those three board members with BlackRock support, it was reported as of October in the Wall Street Journal that the board is considering divesting [Exxon Mobil] of two of their largest overseas projects—one in Mozambique and one in Vietnam—representing north of $30 billion of American investment and know-how that would be put onto the foreign market.[137] And, coincidentally, potentially scooped up by a company like maybe PetroChina, which BlackRock happens to own the equivalent share of interest in, about 6-7%.

And you better believe that if PetroChina gets the opportunity to purchase those assets, should Exxon divest them, Larry Fink will not be voting on[to] any boards of directors of PetroChina [members who] would forego those opportunities. And he wouldn't do that because he's friends with the CCP, but also because the CCP would probably leave him in a ditch somewhere if he did.

The unpatriotic help the likes of Larry Fink are giving to the Communist Chinese as they undermine America is all the more reprehensible as it amounts to rewarding the CCP for avoiding, or simply ignoring, its professed commitment and, in some cases, actual international obligations, to reduce carbon emissions. Given the professed commitment of ESG advocates on Wall Street, their giving the CCP a pass in this way is not just cynical and corrupt. It is contemptible, especially since the result has been unchecked increases in the PRC's output of "greenhouse gases."

Even more egregious is the PRC's bid to be treated as a "developing nation" for the purposes of what amounts to a reparations fund adopted at the 27th Conference of the Parties to the UN Framework Convention on Climate Change (COP 27).[138] This fund amounts to a classic Marxist ploy to redistribute wealth from the countries that purportedly have caused the planet to warm through their intensive burning of fossil fuels to those that claim to have been most adversely affected by the resulting rising temperatures.

Obviously, a Communist China that has the world's second largest economy is *not* a developing country. And the fact that it is generating vast quantities of CO_2 and other greenhouse gases powerfully reinforces the point that *under no circumstances* should the PRC be paid reparations as it does so.

One has, nonetheless, to acknowledge the *chutzpah* "with Chinese characteristics" such a gambit expresses for the United States and the rest of the "developed world." We *deserve* such contempt if we allow the CCP actually to pull off this climate change flim-flam, let alone be rewarded for perpetrating it. David Walsh describes the reality of what is afoot[139]:

> *The goal here is to have, according to the [reparations] committee that's been established [by COP 27], $500-$600 billion a year in transfer payments of this type and then buttressed by later $4-6 trillion-a- year in environmental implementation spending to further remediate the CO_2....Just incredible sums of money.*
>
> *That is indeed a wealth-transfer program and [one] carefully constructed with China's fingerprints all over it due to their being left out of [paying reparations] while they are emitting more CO_2 than all of the other OECD nations combined [and] they would...remain doing that.*
>
> *[Indeed,] Xi Jinping has announced in his energy plans for the next 20 years that coal will be moved from about 60-61% of their energy mix for electricity down to 59[%] "and stabilizing." So, stabilizing means in the mix of coal used in China for generation. So, [the CCP's coal use] is actually going to grow by 7 to 8% a year as their economy grows going forward into the next 20 years.*

Reducing America's Strategic Energy Reserves

In the run-up to the 2022 midterms, the Biden administration sought to reduce gasoline prices that were spiking because of, among other things, its policies aimed at reducing U.S. production and consumption of fossil fuels. To ease such inflation, the U.S. government sold off some 40 percent of the nation's Strategic Petroleum Reserves, leaving the smallest amount since 1984 of oil in the stockpile and available to help contend with and mitigate *authentic* national security crises.

The practical effect is, once again, to increase the vulnerability of the United States and benefit the interests of the Chinese Communist Party. And, in this case, with the Biden administration's blessing, the CCP has actually achieved a two-fer: Its friends have helped draw down oil reserves we may need in a shooting war. And, in the process, the Communist Chinese have humiliated our country by buying directly *for their own emergency reserves* over a million barrels of oil sold off by Team Biden, and an unknown additional amount through cut-outs.[140]

TV host and author Kevin Freeman points out that the pretext used to justify this abuse of America's Strategic Petroleum Reserve is especially outrageous[141]:

> *The Biden energy policy…was enacted specifically to cause higher prices. And that sounds crazy, but that's a part of the Green New Deal. And it is what President Biden campaigned on: canceling the Keystone pipeline; stopping [increased] refining capacity; stopping offshore leases. He promised to end the use of fossil fuels. And one of the features of that is higher prices to cause us to move away from gasoline to electric cars and so forth.*
>
> *Now, he's taken a political[ly] brazen token move to cover this up by pretending the administration cares that gas prices are high.…*
>
> *I believe this is a part of the plan from the Chinese unrestricted warfare perspective, where they are stockpiling oil as we're releasing our stockpile. They're buying it and putting it in their stockpiles. And at the same time, it's harming our domestic energy industry.*

Capt. James Fanell, the former Chief of Intelligence for the U.S. Pacific Fleet, finds it incomprehensible that the Biden administration released oil from the nation's emergency stocks, especially to the CCP, even as it was permanently closing the Navy's only bulk fuel storage facility in Pearl Harbor: "It's just hard to comprehend how you could sell off our Strategic Petroleum Reserve to a nation that's vowed to displace us from the Pacific and to destroy us, and then…shut down our fueling stations in Oahu."[142]

Inside our Wire

Yet another—and particularly alarming—facet of the CCP's energy warfare has been its penetration of America's electric bulk power generation and distribution system, known colloquially as "the grid."

The Center for Security Policy's President and CEO, Lieutenant Colonel Tommy Waller, U.S. Marine Corp (Ret.), observes that such penetration is consistent with China's traditional strategy going back to the time of "Sun Tzu, who wrote that, 'The supreme art of war is to eliminate your enemy, to win without fighting'.…By attacking the electric grid of the United States…the Chinese Communist Party, or really any adversary, could achieve that victory without having to fight us on a battlefield."

Lt. Col. Waller, who leads the Center's Secure the Grid Coalition, notes that there are many ways an enemy like the CCP could take down our grid[143]:

> We know that over the last ten years, there have been more than 700 acts of physical sabotage in the U.S. grid.[144] That's from the utilities reporting it to the Department of Energy. More than 700. That's more than one per week across the country.
>
> Our utility industry is [also] the victim of cyberattacks. Thousands per day.[145] And we know right now that there's malware from state-sponsored cyber hackers from Russia and from China in our grid at the present day. [146] [There is no] requirement, unfortunately, to remove or mitigate that malware.
>
> And then there's electromagnetic attacks [possible in] two ways: 1) directed energy weapons at the localized level, a radio-frequency weapon. And 2) widespread electromagnetic

attack, which would come from a nuclear weapon [detonated] in the atmosphere.

It's notable that all of these types of attacks, particularly EMP and cyber, are in the warfighting doctrine of the Chinese Communist Party.

If all those dangers were not bad enough, Lt. Col. Waller reports that there is "One more threat vector, one that we've…discovered in the last decade, that the Chinese Communist Party has leveraged as part of its unrestricted warfare campaign against the United States. And that's the supply chain."[147]

You've probably seen solar panels and wind turbines and lots of renewables put on the grid. So much of that has been made in China. People don't realize [that] tens of thousands of inverters that transfer that direct current energy into alternating current so we can use it in our homes are made in China and that they can have baked-in vulnerabilities.[148]

In addition, untold numbers of Chinese-produced SKADA systems, computers, chips and other electronic devices are now integrated into the U.S. bulk power system that may well have been designed and configured to be susceptible to cyberattacks, physical sabotage and/or electromagnetic pulses. Taken together with known vulnerabilities in components of the grid manufactured *here* and elsewhere, the CCP's infiltration of our electric infrastructure is an invitation to disaster.

That is especially true of the equipment that is the backbone of today's U.S. electric grid: extra-high-voltage transformers.[149] Lt. Col. Waller puts it this way:

…Perhaps the most worrisome thing that the Chinese have done to attack our supply chain is to manufacture extra high voltage transformers to dump on the…market cheap components and transformer manufacturing in such a way [as] to put American [manufacturers] out of business and own that market space.

Our grid cannot function without these transformers. In 2010 and beforehand, there really wasn't maybe even a single transformer in the U.S. grid that was manufactured in China. Now, we have [hundreds of these] major assets manufactured in China.

...At least one of those was discovered to have a hardware back door.[150] A member of the National Security Council during the Trump administration admitted that that hardware backdoor could have been used to remotely shut down the transformer. It is a safe assumption that the others are similarly rigged to be weaponized against our energy security.

Lt. Col. Waller continues: "So, President Trump in May [2020] declared a grid security emergency. He [issued] an Executive Order that would help to thwart this attack on our supply chain by adversaries like China."[151]

That order was entitled, "Securing the United States Bulk-Power System." According to a Department of Energy press release issued at the time: "The E.O. prohibits Federal agencies and U.S. persons from acquiring, transferring, or installing bulk power system equipment in which any foreign country or foreign national has any interest and the transaction poses an unacceptable risk to national security or the security and safety of American citizens."[152]

Unfortunately, as Lt. Col. Waller says: "On the first day of the Biden administration, that executive order was suspended. And so, the floodgates have now reopened to the Chinese Communist Party." When President Trump issued his Executive Order, there we roughly 300 Chinese extra high voltage transformers inside the wire of the U.S. electrical grid. Since President Biden suspended that order, one hundred more have been allowed in.

The question occurs: Why would President Biden do that? Lt. Col. Waller's answer is as follows:

I have no reasonable explanation for the suspension of that Executive Order for someone whose [responsibility] would be to keep the American people safe. I just have no explanation. The excuse that was given was to, "create a stable policy environment" [in] which the Department of Energy [could] send out a request for information to the industry to ask them how better to [protect the grid]. [That] is, in essence, something we call "kicking the can down the road."

And this is what those in government who are really supposed to be regulating the electric industry properly and those in the Department of Energy—many of them, not all—have been doing for decades. And so, I don't have an answer for how someone who cared about the security of the country would suspend it and not replace it with something better.

American Strategy Group President Brian Kennedy underscores the recklessness of this energy supply chain dependency as follows: "So much of our manufacturing base [is] in China [for] so much of our energy components—whether it's the lithium; lithium ion batteries; or the transformers. The idea that [such equipment] would be made in China is a kind of national madness that Americans just simply need to stop."[153]

In short, the United States has been induced by China's corrupted "Old Friends" on Wall Street, in Washington, at Davos, in official multinational financial and other organizations and in non-governmental ones to pursue a policy towards energy that is profoundly harmful to America's self-sufficiency and national security—and profoundly beneficial to our mortal enemy.

CHARGE 7:
The CCP and Its Enablers Are Taking Down the U.S. Military

The Chinese strategy of "unrestricted warfare" was predicated on the reality that, at the time it was publicly announced with the publication of the two colonels' book in 1999, the People's Liberation Army was no match for the U.S. military. The CCP's purpose in initially and comprehensively using non-kinetic means to weaken America's civilian economy and society was accompanied by two mutually reinforcing lines of attack aimed at altering what the Communists call "the correlation of forces": 1) undermining the United States' armed services and 2) comprehensively building up China's military might. As with every other aspect of Beijing's unrestricted warfare, the help of American elites has been incalculably important to the success of these vectors.

The Waning Might of Our Deterrent

The following have proven to be highly effective in weakening the once-unsurpassed U.S. military:

Ideological Purges and the "Woke" Military:

The Biden administration seized upon what the available evidence increasingly suggests was a premeditated instance of "direct action" on January 6, 2021, to question the loyalty of service personnel deemed to be "white supremacists," "extremists" and potential "domestic terrorists" simply because they are conservatives, constitutionalists, gun-owners and patriots.

Rather than espouse the traditional view that individuals with such characteristics are *precisely* the sort of men and women we want in uniform, the Pentagon under Secretary of Defense Lloyd Austin and Joint Chiefs Chairman General Mark Milley set about applying leftist ideological tests to purge them from the ranks. This wrecking operation began with an emergency stand-down[154] shortly after President Biden's inauguration and continues to this day.

Elaine Donnelly, the founder of the Center for Military Readiness, warns that such purging of so-called "extremists" simply because they are conservatives, while effectively force-feeding the rest of those still in the ranks "anti-extremism" training, is a formula for disaster for the U.S. military.[155]

> *The first thing we had when the new [Biden] administration came in, anti-extremism standards [were] ordered by the Secretary of Defense, Lloyd Austin. How many [man-]hours were spent on this? They actually got a report: It cost 5 million man-hours and over a half million dollars to conduct these stand downs.*
>
> *And guess how many extremists we're talking about? White racists, people who believe in systemic racism—certainly, none of the Antifa types or extremists on the left, only [those] "on the right." You know how many they found? Less than 100.[156] And yet they keep doubling down on these anti-extremism programs. And that is divisive because it goes right into Critical Race Theory.*

Indeed, a key instrument in weeding out of the ranks those deemed to be undesirables has been the relentless imposition on the troops of the Marxist doctrine of Critical Race Theory (CRT).[157, 158] This stratagem for dividing and conquering America condemns all whites as inherently supremacists and oppressors of blacks and other "people of color" and deems all of the latter to be unalterably victims of such racism. It is hard to imagine a program more contrary to the color-blind meritocracy that has been central to the U.S. military's success based on good order and discipline, unit cohesion and combat-effectiveness.

That is precisely the object of the CRT program and why its imposition is so desired by the Chinese Communists and their cultural Marxist allies inside the U.S. government. As Ms. Donnelly points out, that there is no "modern" military—or, for that matter, one in history—that has successfully relied on concepts like diversity, rather than *merit*, to identify and promote competent leaders:

> *Critical Race Theory pits people against each other. How are you supposed to go off to war with somebody who in a CRT*

seminar just accused you of being racist because of the color of your skin? How are you supposed to deal with that?

It's so clearly divisive in any environment, but especially in the armed forces. And yet we know that [in] the service academies, although they've denied it, it has been proven that CRT is becoming endemic.

Among those who have established such proof is retired Air Force Lieutenant General Robert "Rod" Bishop, a founder of and driving force behind Stand Together Against Racism and Radicalism in the Services (STARRS). He recounts the impetus behind the initiation of his organization[159]:

Our organization was founded when we saw the Air Force Academy football coaches put together a video...[where they] chanted "Black Lives Matter" in a militant tone seven times in a three-minute video. So many of us were shocked. What the heck is our alma mater...doing, shouting the slogan of an organization that's told us, "We are Marxists"?

What was even more surprising, however, was the leadership's response to our concerns. "Oh, General Bishop, you don't understand." [I said] "Yeah, I understand....[BLM] has taken a page out of Saul Alinsky's Rules for Radicals, and they're duping half of America and they're taking the U.S. military and apparently you along with it." That was immediately followed by a diversity, equity and inclusion reading room.[160] What's in the [DEI] reading room at the Air Force Academy? All left-wing books. Extreme left-wing books: Malcolm X, Black Panthers....There wasn't any balance.

Unfortunately, similar inroads are being made in other military schools, including the vast Defense Department system for educating dependents' children. The toxic indoctrination thus inflicted on both the troops themselves *and* their kids is contributing to the armed forces' grave shortfalls in retention and recruitment[161, 162] and exacerbating other practices advancing the hollowing out of the services—including the mandating of inoculations for SARS-CoV-2 and serious shortfalls in the defense budget.

COVID "Vaccine" Mandates:

As noted above, an important feature of the "China Model" for responding to the Wuhan Virus pandemic was the mandating of inoculations with so-called COVID "vaccines." It has become increasingly clear that these shots, which actually involve inadequately tested mRNA *gene therapies*, are not only ineffective in protecting healthy military-age men and women. They are actually *dangerous* for many of them.

The toll that has been taken in terms of deaths, serious permanent injuries and serious short-term ones among, for example, pilots has been shockingly severe. Pentagon whistleblower and Air Force flight surgeon Lieutenant Colonel Theresa Long reports that, "After querying all pilots across the [Defense Department] for all-cause morbidity and mortality, I found a stunning increase in the number of reportable events, spiking from an average of 226 reportable events a year (2016-2019) to 4,059 reports in 2022."[163]

Retired Air Force Colonel Robert Maness describes the impact of jab-induced attrition on readiness among his service's pilots[164]:

> *A year ago, we were looking at a 1,650 pilot shortage in the United States Air Force[165], and the vaccine mandate is looking to add another 700 on to that potentially, based on the numbers that we see in the current lawsuits. And it's probably more. That is beyond crisis-level and is a direct impact on the U.S. armed forces readiness.*
>
> *And when you look at military readiness scoring and reporting, you'll see that they're not able to maintain, even today, constant high levels of combat readiness by unit. They have to do what's called "rotating readiness." So, if a unit is not scheduled to deploy or go on a long-term active exercise activity or potential special operations combat drill, they do not do the training at the levels that are required to maintain the highest combat rating.*
>
> *They maintain levels intentionally lower than that because they don't have the time or resources to maintain the levels at the right place. They need to be 24/7. That is totally different than what the American armed forces were capable of doing just ten years ago.*

Such reduced readiness would be undesirable at any time. If, however, the Commander of the Air Mobility Command, Air Force four-star General Mike Minihan, is right in his prediction[166] that we will be in a shooting war with the Chinese Communist Party by 2025, such unpreparedness can condemn us to certain defeat. The General is to be commended for ordering his subordinates to heighten their readiness and training against that eventuality. But he and other squared-away military personnel are being undermined by the CCP and its friends in this country.

That is particularly true insofar as the Biden administration has, by compelling service personnel to take "the jab" and disallowing exceptions on grounds of personal conscience or religious belief, secured a "two-fer" that goes far beyond degrading readiness: The U.S. military has driven out of its ranks many of those who refused to be "vaccinated" and, in the process, identified and furthered its purge of those who likely have what it considers to be undesirable ideological views, as well—but who would be particularly prized if the shooting war with the CCP of which General Minihan warns actually eventuates.

Eviscerating the Defense Budget:

As noted above, the Biden team's reckless disregard for budgetary discipline has created inflation on a scale unseen in decades. Among the most severely impacted by such erosion in purchasing power are the armed forces, whose budgets assumed an inflation rate of 2 percent, instead of the 8+ percent that is actually being experienced.[167] That translates into acute shortfalls, particularly in training, operations and maintenance, research and modernization programs.

Even before Joe Biden's inflation began taking its toll, America's armed services were being seriously underfunded in terms of: the acquisition of planes, ships, missiles and other materiel; rigorous training for combat; heightened operational tempo; and other priorities made more urgent by the burgeoning Chinese threat.

The cumulative effect of these fiscal and the aforementioned ideological and vax mandate assaults on the morale, character and condition of America's armed forces has been: dramatically to deplete those forces with the loss of large numbers of highly trained and combat-tested servicemen and women; the failure to attract sufficient numbers of recruits to meet the services' minimum goals, let alone offset the attrition taking place at the moment; and an increasingly debilitating loss of confidence in the military's leadership, both uniformed and civilian.

These developments not only undermine the readiness and effectiveness of the United States' military posture. They may actually *invite aggression* by China. As the former Chief of Intelligence of the U.S. Pacific Fleet, retired Navy Captain James Fanell, well knows, the Chinese are closely monitoring and taking stock of what the U.S. is doing to its armed forces[168]:

> *The Chinese Communist Party analyzes things through [the] lens of "Comprehensive National Power" (CNP), and there are 98 million members of the Chinese Communist Party [who] are constantly analyzing CNP data that comes in.*
>
> *…So, they're going to look at that [data about our military's condition] and they're going to run it through their computers and they're going to say: "Well, this could be the best time"….I think between now and 2025 is when an invasion [of Taiwan] could occur.*
>
> *And given the domestic political situation in the United States and the likelihood that there may be a swing back to a presidency that's clearly going to confront the Chinese Communist Party, China may decide that they have to move before that person can get in and make changes.*

Of course, the CCP's calculations of the risks associated with *going for it* are a function of not only the perceived declining power of our armed forces, but the changing "correlation of forces" reflecting as well the CCP's decades-long build-up of its own arsenal and other steps it has been taking to increase decisively the PRC's Comprehensive National Power.

The Intensified PLA Challenge

The Chinese Communist Party has made a top priority of amassing the capability fully to dominate its immediate region. It has also greatly progressed towards having the various means required to project power globally. This reality is evident not only in the accumulation of ever more and increasingly capable ships, missiles, aircraft and other weaponry. It is also reflected in the vast industrial capability now in place to build such armaments and otherwise support the missions on land, air, sea and space in which they might be used.

The CCP's Nuclear Buildup:

To cite but one illustrative, and particularly troubling, example: The CCP is making great strides in achieving nuclear superiority over us by putting into place a comprehensively modernized strategic Triad.[169] It is on track to be considerably larger than the U.S. nuclear arsenal, which is now—and will for years to come be—comprised of very old, and in some cases utterly obsolescent, weapons. In addition, China now has fielded first-strike-capable hypersonic missiles for which we currently have no counterpart or in-kind deterrent.[170]

A leading expert on China's military, Richard Fisher, characterizes the CCP's ominous nuclear force structure this way[171]:

> *The Dongfeng 41 (DF-41) mobile ICBM—and presumably also silo-launched and rail-launched…is said to have three warheads.…But for over a decade, Chinese sources have been saying this [missile] is capable of carrying ten warheads.*
>
> *Now, based on these numbers, what we know and what has been recently revealed about Chinese nuclear ballistic missile submarines—apparently they have all been upgraded with the new JL-3 submarine launched ballistic missile.…By 2035, China could be deploying about 1500 nuclear warheads, roughly the same number as the United States and Russia deploy today.*
>
> *[In addition,] China has been spending the last two years building at least 360 new [missile] silos in its western desert. And these 360 silos are going to be armed with an ICBM [at least] as capable as the DF 41. Now, with that number of new ICBMs and with three warheads, China could in those fields alone, deploy 1080 new warheads. Now you add the JL-3, which is also said to have three warheads. You're*

already reaching a total of nearly 1300 warheads....And the [Pentagon's 2022] PLA report says today that China has a stockpile of 400 warheads.

I don't expect that China is going to take another 12 years to deploy all these warheads. I expect that these warheads will be deployed within the next 1 to 2 years. And that the number of Chinese warheads...will surpass the number of American deployed warheads at about that time.

In the wake of the Chinese surveillance balloon's overflight of key U.S. strategic assets and bases in early 2023, Mr. Fisher added:

This balloon was an inner space satellite....It had a much more refined ability to gather information about the weather over the American missile and bomber bases. Why is this important? Because when you fire a maneuverable warhead—especially a small warhead, or more importantly, China's new hypersonic glide vehicles—having knowledge of the weather over the target is extremely important. The weather can affect tremendously the accuracy of those warheads, especially when you're trying to hit a target as small as an ICBM silo.

And this raises my second major point. The balloon, combined with the already massive Chinese geostationary, deep space early warning satellite...all point, to me, to the beginning of a Chinese transition from doctrines of defense and deterrence to doctrines of warfighting, to include massive first strikes.[172]

To make matters worse, former Defense Department official and author Dr. Matthew Kroenig notes[173], "As China greatly expands its arsenal, for the first time in U.S. history, the United States is going to have to face *two* near-peer nuclear powers, Russia and China, at the same time. And...that will require increasing the size of our arsenal. But how are we going to do that? It won't be easy."

In addition, Beijing has invested unimaginable sums in putting into place a host of other capabilities relevant to nuclear warfighting. Among them are: myriad bunkers for assuring the survival of regime leaders, party cadres and key production facilities and workers; *3,000 miles* of tunnels designed to protect and conceal mobile ballistic missiles and other assets; air and missile defenses; and hardened silos, aircraft shelters and submarine bases. Apart from the old silos in its Minuteman III missile fields, the United States has few, if any, counterparts to such defenses.

Moreover, taken together, the CCP's nuclear build-up and its immense investment over the years in strategic defenses bespeak an increasingly ominous Communist Chinese attachment to the belief that the CCP can fight and win a nuclear war with the United States.[174] We must act now to disabuse Xi and his minions of that possibility.

Lest there be any doubt, there is no reason to believe that the CCP will agree to negotiate away any of these capabilities that are enabling Communist China to achieve decisive advantages over us. One of America's most experienced national security practitioners/arms control negotiators, Ambassador Robert Joseph, observes[175]:

> *I think it's clear to everyone that Beijing has absolutely no interest in participating in any arms control negotiations that would lead to any constraints on their massive nuclear buildup. China has rejected all calls to do so. China has also, through its actions and through its words, made clear that it is not willing to consider any measures that would provide for effective verification.*
>
> *And even if that were not the case—even if they did engage in negotiations and made commitments for monitoring and inspections—looking at their record of violations with the Chemical Weapons Convention and the Biological Weapons Convention, [and indeed,] almost any agreement that they've signed up to, they violated each and every one of them. And the same would, I think, clearly be the case for any future agreement regarding nuclear weapons.*

"Whole-of-Society":

Another factor in China's significantly surpassing the United States with respect to their respective Comprehensive National Power scores is the CCP's *whole-of-society* approach to marshalling the PRC's people and resources and subordinating them to meeting the needs of the People's

Liberation Army. The entirety of the PRC's businesses, academic institutions, the workforce writ large and, of course, the Chinese Communist Party is working to defeat the United States of America and achieve Xi Jinping's China Dream, namely global domination.

Preeminent China expert Gordon G. Chang describes the motivation for such a societal mobilization, and what it entails, this way[176]:

> *Xi Jinping is preparing for war. We know that he's engaged in the fastest military buildup since the Second World War. He's trying to sanction-proof his regime. And most ominously, he is mobilizing China's civilians and companies for war. And this is the question of civil-military fusion. It's not just the military companies. It's all companies. Because under this doctrine of civil-military fusion, the military has access to everything that civilian companies have. So that is the ultimate reality. It doesn't matter, all these issues of how we might define "war." We know that China is prepared for battle....We are not responding. So, what does this mean? It means that America is on the eve of perhaps the greatest tragedy in our history.*

Three other manifestations of the CCP's unbridled mobilization of the Chinese motherland warrant brief mention: The Party's unprecedentedly comprehensive espionage operations; its mobilization of ethnic Fifth Columns among overseas Chinese and their descendants; and its preparations for war in and from outer space.

Intelligence Warfare:

Career intelligence professional and CPDC member Nicholas Eftimiades calls to mind a striking analogy to capture the all-encompassing nature of China's approach to intelligence collection[177]:

> *The FBI...said if the Russians were trying to steal a bucket of sand, they would land a sub at night, a bunch of commandos would get out of the sub, go to the shore, get a bucket of sand, row back to the sub and disappear under the waves in the night. China [would send] ten thousand bathers the next day and everyone would just dust some sand off themselves when they got home. And that's the way they approach intelligence. It's*

"People's intelligence," as Mao called it. *It's intelligence on a massive scale.*

Nick Eftimiades describes China's comprehensive approach to intelligence as "target[ing] multiple aspects of American society, technology, critical infrastructure as well as government, and, in an extraordinary fashion, [employing] the Chinese diaspora [including] in cases of influence which China conducts…on a scale unseen in human history":

> *They do that through what they call a process of "encirclement"….*
> *They're looking towards a political figure and…recruiting academics, recruiting business persons, recruiting people around that individual…to try and influence that person, to change the course of direction of a government or policies.*

> *So, there's this entire covert influence component going on, much of which involves Chinese intelligence, trying to manipulate the United States government, foreign governments and societies as a whole.*

> *Then, you have the theft of technology. Again, trillions of dollars [in] total, hundreds of billions-a-year in technology stolen by China. And it's not just by intelligence officers. You can say that's the nexus, the center of it, but that expands out into state-owned enterprises. And in China, just at the national level there are 50,000 of [such collectors]. It extends to the use of [what passes for "private sector"] companies. It extends to the use of individuals.*

> *And the Chinese legal system makes sure that those companies, enterprises and*

> *individuals…comply. So, we have an extraordinary permeation of society that's done, all with the intent of derailing the society [and] destroying, or certainly derailing, democracy….So the intelligence services play a critical role in [all of] this.*

Weaponizing the Chinese Diaspora:

Mr. Eftimiades notes that the CCP uses overseas Chinese to affect the correlation of forces. As we will discuss further in Charge 8 in connection with the Chinese Communists' political warfare against this country, in the words of Dr. Sean Lin, a survivor of Tiananmen Square and former U.S. Army virologist, the practice of compelling the Chinese diaspora to help the motherland is widely employed by the Party[178]:

> We need to understand the Chinese government quite often use[s expatriates'] connection with China as leverage to force Chinese people to support the Chinese government. For example, many people may have business in China. We may have family members, relatives inside China. The government [threatens] many Chinese-Americans [saying], "If you have any criticisms on the Chinese government, you may not be able to continue your business in China." "You may not have a free talk with your family members in China. Those talks may be monitored by the Chinese government." Or all kinds of [other] threats. So, they coerce many Chinese American people to support the government.

China's Ambitions in Space:

There may be no more strategically impactful example of the CCP's civil-military fusion than its efforts to bend the whole of its society and nominally "civilian" space program to advance PRC domination of the high frontier. Richard Fisher has closely studied this facet, among many others, of the Chinese Communists' efforts to take down the United States and its armed forces. He describes the Party's three major ambitions in space and its employment of "unrestricted warfare" in that domain as follows[179]:

> First, the Chinese Communist Party seeks dominance in low-Earth orbit, mainly to be able to win wars on the Earth. Secondly, the Chinese Communist Party seeks dominance over the Earth-Moon and Earth-Moon-Mars systems. This is essentially to lock in the Chinese Communist Party's ambition for hegemony on Earth.

And then at a third level, the Chinese Communist Party is developing, unfolding and conducting a very ambitious program for conducting research, becoming aware of what is in deep space. That is the future high ground. And the Chinese Communist Party does not want to be outflanked by any other power, especially the United States.

The CCP also wants to control the Lagrangian points, points within the Earth-Moon system of equidistant gravitational pull. It would be convenient to station manned or unmanned space stations [at such locations in space] to try to contain or at least deny access within the Earth-Moon system to other powers.

China also wants to go to Mars. The Long March-9 will probably be the first vehicle that it will use to go to Mars.... But beyond Mars, China is investing in deep space. They want to try to go and land on an asteroid, bring back a sample of the surface of an asteroid, because they understand, like we do, like our allies, that asteroids are going to be a major source of future resources for consumption on Earth. China has plans to go to the moons of Jupiter. It has plans to go out to Neptune and probably beyond.

Alliances: Weakening Ours, Strengthening Theirs:

The Chinese Communist Party has another, yin-yang technique aimed at changing the correlation of forces to its advantage. As Cleo Paskal, a Foundation for Defense of Democracy Fellow and expert on Chinese penetration of the South Pacific and South Asia, puts it[180]: "You can improve your Comprehensive National Power two ways: One is kind of the American competitive way, which is you get better. The other is you knock the other side down."

To those ends, the CCP has been using a combination of carrots and sticks—influence operations, bribes, Belt and Road pay-day loans, seizure of and construction on South China Sea atolls claimed by other nations and actual overt threats—to fracture America's alliances and induce our partners to seek accommodations with Beijing. Ms. Paskal observes[181]:

China wants to be Number One in the world, in terms of Comprehensive National Power. And it is incredibly comprehensive. It's a definition that the sort of Middle Kingdom [of] all under heaven, all this all refers back to China, whether it's intellectual property or economics or military power, social power, cultural power, geographical access. It's…all encompassed in this Comprehensive National Power push out. And they are very good at figuring out weaknesses in our system.

Once you start to look at Comprehensive National Power and the unrestricted warfare that supports it, you can see there are all these sorts of things that we aren't doing—and that there are other countries that maybe we could look at. For example, India. India has managed to reclaim the Maldives from the grips of the Chinese Communist Party through a comprehensive multinational defense, or pushback, [against] the [CCP's] Comprehensive National Power attempts at using elite capture in order to get in the country.

At the same time the Chinese Communists are working to undermine our alliances, they are strengthening and exercising leadership of *their* alliances, notably, those with Russia, North Korea, Pakistan and Iran. They are also effectively colonizing those among the Belt and Road partner nations who can be strategically helpful in making any conflict with the United States truly global in character.

Mobilizing and Weaponizing the Chinese People:

Particularly ominous in terms of China's growing Comprehensive National Power is the evidence that the CCP is now preparing its society and people for *kinetic* war with the United States and its allies. The Center for Security Policy's Director of China Policy, Dr. Bradley Thayer, points out that, in the wake of the CCP's 20th Party Congress in October 2022, Xi's aggressive intentions have been made explicit. These are[182]:

First, China is set to take over running the world, which is the realization of [Xi's] ambition for the Chinese Communist Party to be the dominant force in the international politics, to set the norms, rules, regulations and standards of international politics, and to bend international institutions to the will of the CCP....

Second, Xi was steadfast in that the ideology of the CCP remains firmly anchored in Marxism-Leninism-Maoism, the guiding rule for the Party as he interprets it. And he is a steadfast believer in Communism and seeks to strengthen the ideological purity of the CCP while strengthening its control over China and the rest of the world.

And then thirdly, belligerence was the order of the day and [Xi's] address. And as we've witnessed in the wake of the [Party] Congress, his aggressive discourse was directed against the U.S. in [the] denunciation of what he called "hegemony" and, implicitly, U.S. allies like Japan and partners like India.

Most explicitly, however, Xi's aggressive intent was directed against Taiwan, where he stated that resolving the Taiwan question is a matter for the Chinese and must be resolved by [them], and the use of force will never be renounced in that context. So, the implication is that coercive measures against Taiwan are going to intensify, most likely in the near term.

As noted elsewhere, manifestations of the war-footing Xi is demanding include: video-taped evidence of Beijing-ordered planning meetings at the provincial level to prepare the home front for conflict; constriction of supply chains to the United States and others; hoarding of food, medicine, fertilizers and critical materials; Zero-Covid lockdowns that can, among other things, demonstrate the sort of sacrifice and discipline war will require; heightened propaganda against the United States and others portrayed as enemies of China; and intensified offensive military operations against Taiwan; and heightened activity in the South China and East China seas (including joint air and naval exercises with Russia).

If no other Charge in this Indictment were grounds for action against the Chinese Communist Party, the fact that it is now a formidable and *probably imminent* source of violent conflict against this country and its friends, allies and vital interests should suffice.

The adverse evolution of the U.S.-China correlation of forces is even more ominous in light of the growing prospect that the PLA's threatening capabilities may be augmented by Russia's, as well. Taken together, all these factors are inexorably translating into: a dangerously "hollowed out" and misled U.S. military; a Chinese Communist Party that is both emboldened and increasingly in trouble at home; an abundantly armed and trigger-happy People's Liberation Army; and a time of testing made all the more fraught by two more examples of the CCP's unrestricted warfare against America: its political warfare and information operations.

CHARGE 8:
The CCP Is Waging 'Divide-and-Conquer' Political Warfare against America

As we have discussed above, the Chinese Communist Party has built on ancient stratagems going back to the great military theoretician Sun Tzu's insights, to hone the practice of fostering fault lines within its enemies' camps. It has, moreover, relentlessly exploited such divisions so as to fracture and defeat such foes, preferably without fighting.

In addition to the foregoing lines of unrestricted warfare attack, the CCP has, both directly and through its ideological allies, United Front proxies and captured elites in this country, employed the following political warfare techniques as part of its efforts to destroy America:

Cultural Marxism:

Mao Tse-tung weaponized what he called "Cultural Revolution" as a means of wresting and consolidating power at the expense of his CCP rivals. It mobilized young Communists of the Red Guard to use "class warfare" to attack, publicly humiliate and destroy—in many cases, literally—Party leaders and other officials, members of the professional elite and so-called bourgeoisie, land-owners and anyone else deemed to be anti-Mao or an impediment to the realization of his revolutionary goals.

Marxists in America have been coached and otherwise encouraged by their sponsors in Beijing to use racial, instead of class, divisions to weaken and subvert this country. It is not an accident that Black Lives Matter—the prime-mover behind the so-called 2020 "Summer of Love" race-riots across the country—has been sponsored and promoted by Liberation Road, a CCP-tied spin-off of the Maoist Freedom Road Socialist Organization.[183]

The Black Lives Matter movement has also propelled the establishment and enforcement of "hate speech" laws in multiple states across the nation. These statutes are particularly suited to suppressing a prime target of the Marxists: people of faith. Trevor Loudon, who co-produced a documentary called *Enemies Within the Church*,[184] credits

Liberation Road and the Communist Party USA with being the prime drivers behind hate speech legislation and the official characterization of "Christian nationalists" and, most recently, "radical traditional Catholics" (RTCs) as domestic violent extremists (DVEs)[185]:

> Most states now have hate speech legislation. Now, hate speech legislation is a tool of the Communists to suppress opposition. It has nothing to do with tolerance. It's quite the opposite....I've watched this come out of the left—out of Liberation Road and Freedom Road and the Communist Party USA.

> [They] all started pushing this Christian nationalist theme meme about a year ago. Now the president's talking about it. Now senators are talking about it.

> It comes from China. It goes to the left. The left make it mainstream. So, you don't know it's China. You don't know it's maybe Russian influence or Cuban influence. You don't know that. You just see Democrats talking about this and unions talking about it and academics talking about it.

> But if you follow it back, it comes out of the Communist movement and the Communist movement takes its cues from America's enemies. So, we are seeing the "othering" of Christians, but not just Christians, anybody who stands against the regime....We are in a revolution. And too many Americans don't even understand that fact.

Othering:

Totalitarians—and especially Communists like Lenin, Stalin and Mao—reflexively seek to marginalize their opponents as a vehicle to turn the public against them and, in due course, render them utterly incapable of resistance to the state, the party and its leader.

Dr. Michael Rectenwald brings to the topic the authority of a former Marxist professor at New York University and author of a number of highly relevant books, including *Thought Criminal*[186]. It describes his experiences when he dared to question the behavior of his colleagues, administrators and students. In short order, they turned on and ultimately drove him from his university post. Having been "othered" himself, he describes the practice as follows[187]:

> *Othering is a way of alienating a person and or a body of people from the legitimate body of citizens. It's a way of casting them aside. They become an object thrown out and as such, demonized, vilified and even criminalized.... It is a very typical ploy of a totalitarian regime. Which I think is what we're up against, actually.*

> *This is what they do: Once they take power, usually through revolutionary coup, they have to expel their enemies because these enemies represent a threat to their illegitimate power. And they make all crimes political crimes. And the only kind of crime you can commit is actually a political crime. They typically let their own followers, their own contingent, run rampant over the population and deem their crimes to be legal.*

Dede Laugesen, the Committee on the Present Danger: China's Executive Secretary, cites Don Hanle's analysis in his book *Terrorism: The Newest Face of Warfare*[188] to map in more detail how a perpetrator of othering—an "identity entrepreneur"—sets the stage for isolation, subjugation and, in extreme cases, destruction[189]:

> *First, the identity entrepreneur identifies an "other" and starts explaining how this "other" is a problem and using this threat to gain power. In the second step, the "other" is dehumanized, made to be cast in doubt and dispersion. Then, the "other" is stripped of their rights, first socially and then in law. And once that happens, the "other" is disarmed and the killing and the violence begins.*

Dr. Rectenwald warns that President Biden's notorious "Red Speech"[190] before Independence Hall September 1, 2022 had ominous hallmarks of othering[191]:

> *We're looking at Biden standing before [Independence] Hall and with a red light beaming and unequivocal appearance of hellfire and glowing gloves of military officers standing behind him, which to me suggests two things. One, and this goes in*

conjunction with what he said, but the thing that it suggested to me is that his political opposition can expect hellfire—that they can expect to be treated to a kind of damnation by the political establishment. And the military installation behind him, the two officers—one whose glove was rather inordinately glowing—seem to suggest to me that military force was not out of the question in suppressing this dissident contingent of the population.

…He declared that, "MAGA Republicans represent a threat to the Republic." And then, as such, that they are basically beyond the pale of political representation. They should not be considered a legitimate political contingent. They should be isolated. They should be shunned. They should be othered. They should be effectively cordoned off and deemed completely illegitimate and even criminal. This comes from studying the history of Communist regimes in the Soviet Union, China and elsewhere. And everything about this speech was very typical [of such regimes]

Dede Laugesen concludes that[192]:

Biden is demonizing America's conservatives, Christians and others who hold traditional conservative views.…The rhetoric in America pertaining to conservatives and specifically conservative Christians is increasingly inflammatory and discriminatory. Parents protesting critical race theory, "gender fluidity," LGBTQ rights, pornography and other various Team Biden political agendas imposed on public school children have been called domestic extremists and threatened with prosecution by America's top law enforcement officer, Merrick Garland[193].…

The net result of "othering" is division, exclusion, deception and violent death. Techniques used in the process of othering force individuals to question their dignity and police their own thoughts in a drive to negate personal liberty and subject every individual to the power of the accusing authority. In China, this authority is the Communist Party. In America, it's Team Biden and the radical left.

In Xi's China, nothing—not family, not religion, nor any other institution—is allowed to stand between the individual and the all-encompassing power of the state. In CCP-like fashion, Team Biden and Big Tech are working together to restrict free speech and increase population control and surveillance. They don't even hide it.

> *Welcome to Mao's Cultural Revolution, now being waged in America.*

Attacks on America's families:

Reggie Littlejohn, the founder and president of Women's Rights Without Frontiers, characterizes as follows why the practice of undermining "nuclear" and extended families is central to totalitarian ideologies[194]:

> *Karl Marx in the Communist Manifesto called for the abolition of the family. Why would Communism require the abolition of the family? It's because it's in the family that we draw our strength to confront evil.*
>
> *And if you can break those relationships—if you can break the relationship between husband and wife, if you can break the bond between mother and child, if you can bring break the bonds between parents and children—then you can isolate people. You can terrify them, and you can completely decimate the structure of society.*
>
> *Totalitarianism depends on the isolation of people, on the atomization of society…and the elevation of the government as the locus of love and loyalty for everyone. So nowhere has this process been implemented with more force or diabolical success than by China.*

Xi Van Fleet, a survivor of Mao Tse-Tung's Cultural Revolution explains how China's first Communist dictator prioritized and practiced his anti-family initiatives[195]:

> *The first killing [of Mao's Cultural Revolution] happened in…a girls' middle school in Beijing.…The assistant principal was killed by a bunch of girls as young as 12. How could that*

happen? How could those young girls turn into monsters? That's because [of] the breaking down of the Chinese family that the CCP had been implementing for decades before the Cultural Revolution.

So, in the traditional Chinese culture, and it's founded on Confucianism, and one of the core [tenets] of Confucius teaching is the filial piety, and that is basically teaching people to be loyal to your family, to respect your parents and take care of them when they are old. And Mao did not want that. He want[ed] the loyalty to him and to [the] CCP. So, when I was very young—and this happened to all Chinese children—we were taught that even though our parents gave birth to us, our real parents are the Party.

In accordance with the doctrine of Marxist and Maoist Communism, breaking familial bonds in America has been a central thrust of today's cultural revolution here.

For example, in a 2015 video, Patrisse Cullors, one of the co-founders of Black Lives Matter declared that she is a "trained Marxist."[196] Not coincidentally, her organization's website for a time professed on its "What We Believe" page: "We disrupt the Western-prescribed nuclear family structure requirement."[197]

Symptoms of this assault by the CCP and its friends in this country include the indoctrination of children in what are properly depicted as "government schools." This involves the compulsory embrace of radical leftist nostrums and agendas—many of which are anathema to the parents involved and generally inflicted without their knowledge.

Among these, as noted above, are the use of racism-focused cultural warfare via: the promotion of Critical Race Theory and its allegations of unalterable inequality and victimhood; teaching that the United States is systemically racist, ditto its founders and their Constitution; and that, therefore, its history must be reviled and repudiated. These forces are also subversively promoting transgenderism and climate alarmism to further radicalize and fracture especially younger Americans.

In addition, the CCP has inflicted incalculable harm on American families and their society *directly* by murdering over a 100,000 thousand of us in the last year alone with chemical warfare in the form of fentanyl manufactured in China or in Mexico using Chinese-supplied ingredients. That loss of life is twice the number killed in the eight years of war in Vietnam. It has been likened to the death-toll of a fully loaded 747 crash *every day*.

Chinese officials have repeatedly promised to end this practice but have yet to do so. They seem, instead, bent on selling *more* of this murderous drug here than ever. In fact, last year, the Drug Enforcement Agency seized enough fentanyl to kill every man, woman in child in America.[198]

The Center for Immigration Studies' National Security Analyst, Todd Bensman, is the author of *America's Covert Border War*[199] and *Overrun: How Joe Biden Unleashed the Greatest Border Crisis in U.S. History*[200] and one of the most indefatigable, intrepid and courageous monitors of Joe Biden's border crisis. He reports that[201]:

> China has been a primary source for the precursor chemicals that are necessary to the manufacturing process of fentanyl.... The Chinese are not sending fentanyl—the deadly poison that has killed about 110,000 Americans in a year or so[202]....But they provide the precursor chemicals to the Mexican cartels that have laboratories in the big cities and sometimes in the rural areas where they're producing the fentanyl.
>
> They couldn't produce this fentanyl without those precursor chemicals that are coming in by port and by air from Chinese proxy countries without Chinese assent.
>
> The Chinese government has agreed to control those precursor chemicals, or to try to control those precursor chemicals. They agreed to do that in 2018. And we see how that's turned out.
>
> My feeling about that is that the Chinese probably are profiting financially, whoever the companies are, that are providing the chemicals into Mexico. But they also probably willfully want to create havoc in American society, to kind of tear our fabric to cause problems for us through this drug. Certainly, if they were

an ally, they would be working very closely with us to halt the sources of the precursor. But that is not happening.

Then, there is the toll on families associated with the Chinese Communists' biological warfare attack described in Charge 4 above. The loss of over a million Americans ascribed to the Wuhan Virus is but one measure of such costs. There are many other adverse impacts, including: children being locked out of schools, denied socialization, prevented from seeing the faces of their parents, teachers and classmates, and forced to engage in less effective "remote learning"; families estranged and/or unable to be with loved ones due to vaccination-related considerations; and families unable to attend services in their houses of worship.

Attack on the Church:

The Chinese Communist Party is not simply atheistic. It is Satanic. Terrified of the popularity of the Christian church in China—which is said to have more adherents than the CCP has members, it has gone to extreme lengths at home to suppress Christians and, for that matter, members of other faith communities (notably, Falun Gong, Tibetan Buddhists and Uyghur and other Muslim minorities). With help from Pope Francis in the form of a secret agreement ceding considerable authority over the Catholic church's operations in China, Xi Jinping has substituted his cult of personality for Christian teachings and traditions. For example, in 2019, the Ten Commandments have been removed and replaced with quotes by Xi Jinping.[203]

International child rights lawyer and Vatican watchdog Elizabeth Yore describes a particularly diabolical manifestation of the Chinese Communists' war on faith,[204] namely the CCP's use of restrictions on children's participation in religious services[205]:

> *In 2018, the CCP and the Chinese government declared that religion is dangerous for minors. All children under the age of 18 [are prohibited] from participating in any religious activities. And the god that they are [told] to worship is…Xi Jinping. No child in China is allowed to go to church [or] to participate in summer camps' religious activities. In fact, the Open Doors [USA 2022][206] report on religious persecution in China said that we are going to lose the next generation of Christians.*

Marxists in the United States have been no less assiduous in their efforts to subvert and destroy the Church here. "The United States was the very first country in the world founded on the principle that man's rights come from God, not the government," says Trevor Loudon.[207] "And that offended every tyrant, every king, every dictator, every Communist across the face of the planet."

Hence, as noted above, the leftists in the U.S. government have branded "Christian nationalists" and "radical Catholic traditionalists" as domestic extremists.[208] Communists have taken over many American seminaries and undermined the theology and civic role traditionally promoted by such institutions. They have made great strides in neutralizing Christian pastors and congregations in this country, as well, both with respect to their historic beliefs and values and their leadership in preserving our constitutional Republic.[209]

For instance, the radical left in government at all levels seized upon the opportunity presented by the COVID pandemic and the China Model response to it to lockdown churches and other places of worship—and found willing collaborators in doing so in many denominations and faiths.

Open Border:

The Chinese Communist Party's strategy of dividing and weakening the United States has benefitted greatly from President Biden's destruction of this nation's borders, especially its southern one with Mexico. As noted above, the CCP has entered into lucrative money-laundering, fentanyl-smuggling and human-trafficking partnerships with the Mexican drug cartels. Chinese nationals are among the millions who have come here illegally in recent years and effectively, if not officially, gained asylum. It would be recklessly naïve to believe that Communist Party cadres and People's Liberation Army operatives are not among the million or more other recent illegal immigrants that have "gotten away" by avoiding the relatively few Border Patrol or other law enforcement personnel as are still monitoring illegal penetrations of the frontier. What could possibly go wrong?

Of particular concern to former Texas Department of Public Safety intelligence analyst Todd Bensman are the agents of Chinese intelligence gaining access to our country this way[210]:

One issue that I frequently raise about the Chinese coming across that border and about the open border in general is the threat of espionage….The Chinese have been sending us spies through the J Visa program and the F Visa programs—that's the cultural exchange program and the student visa program— ad nauseum for years and years. And we've been catching them by the dozen coming through on those programs [as] there is a heightened American counter-espionage program that is aimed at the J and F visas.[211]

And with that pressure on those visas, it behooves Chinese intelligence to send…them [here] through an easier way, which is over the border. They don't say anything except "I want asylum," and then they're in to set up shop however they want.

Election Interference:

The Chinese Communist Party had a powerful incentive to help prevent President Donald Trump's reelection and to achieve the victory in his stead of a candidate who they are said to regard as a "controlled asset."

A November 2020 video by the Committee on the Present Danger: China entitled, *Seeding the Vote: China's Influence in the 2020 U.S. General Election*[212] revealed the Chinese Communist Party funded U.S. groups to influence the outcome of that year's controversial elections.

Foreign interference in U.S. elections is illegal. Yet, in January 2021 Cardiff University reported a sophisticated China-linked social media operation played a key role in spreading disinformation during and after the 2020 U.S. election.[213] Researchers also found evidence of the same network spreading anti-U.S. propaganda that amplified calls for violence before and after the Capitol riot in Washington on January 6, 2021. Professor Martin Innes, Director of the Crime and Security Research Institute, who leads its Open Source Communications Analytics Research (OSCAR) team says[214]:

…Our analysis using open-source traces strongly suggests multiple [social media operations] links to China. Our initial findings suggested that the operation was not especially complex, but as we have dug deeper into the network, we have

had to substantially revise our original view. The behavior of the accounts was sophisticated and disciplined, and seemingly designed to avoid detection by Twitter's countermeasures. There is at least one example of these accounts helping to propagate disinformation that went on to receive more than a million views.

While the full extent of Chinese interference in the 2020 presidential race may never be known, one thing is sure: The Wuhan Virus Beijing unleashed on this country and the China Model it promoted as a response created the conditions that resulted in states across the country adopting deeply problematic mail-in balloting procedures. The results appear to have borne out the warning in 2005 by a bipartisan commission co-chaired by former President Jimmy Carter and former White House Chief of Staff James Baker that, "Absentee ballots remain the largest source of potential voter fraud."[215]

Other techniques available to a CCP determined to interfere in the 2020 election and, for that matter, the subsequent 2022 midterms appear to include: cyberwarfare facilitated by software and internet access to U.S. election machines; access to data reportedly housed on servers in China concerning American election personnel and voter rolls; and voter registration drives in swing states run by non-governmental organizations with ties to the CCP front groups and their funding.

Deep divisions between the political parties and their voters arising from concerns about election integrity have greatly intensified the combined effects of the other facets of a divide-and-conquer strategy assiduously pursued by the Chinese Communists and their enablers here. They have been further inflamed by the CCP's extensive information operations described in Charge 9.

CHARGE 9:
The CCP Is Attacking America with Subversive Information Operations

The Chinese Communist Party makes relentless use of a wide variety of information warfare instruments as part of its unrestricted warfare against the United States. Like the other techniques employed for that purpose, CCP information and influence operations have as their goal subverting and ultimately destroying America. They are extremely hostile acts that reinforce the peril we are facing and should be understood, *and responded to*, as such.

Author and essayist Benjamin Weingarten describes the object of Chinese information operations as follows[216]:

> *"Document Number Nine" from the Chinese Communist Party, which was cast early on under Xi's tenure...basically says that our [American] ideals, our founding values and principles pose an existential threat to the CCP regime. Consequently, it has to engage in mass censorship of those views [at home] while at the same time exporting its own to combat those views in a foreign context. And this is all part and parcel of an effort to be the hegemonic world power and to promote its favored narratives and block our favorite narratives—or at least what ought to be our favored narratives because they're rooted in truth....*

Weingarten describes the cumulative effects of allowing such false Chinese narratives to go uncontested, citing as an example the notorious meeting in Alaska in March 2021[217], during which Secretary of State Blinken and National Security Advisor Sullivan failed to push back as their Chinese counterparts trash-talked the United States:

> *...It showed that...our purported leaders...were submitting to the narrative that the Chinese Communist Party put forth, that we are somehow immoral, that America was conceived in sin.... The Chinese Communist Party and, of course, Communists have for decades propagated the narratives that are today*

propagated by our progressive elites. But they were playing on those elites, exploiting their own self-doubt and lack of moral clarity. And so, consequently, we see convergence in narratives between our elites and Chinese Communist Party elites.

Of course, a truly American administration would have responded by slapping the Chinese Communist Party as being the greatest human rights violators arguably in the history of mankind, and that they had no business even raising the term "human rights" in the first place. But of course, instead, our administration said, "You know, we take umbrage with that characterization. America has worked hard, but we haven't fulfilled our greatest values and principles," etc., etc. That should never be the answer of an American representative.

Examples of the myriad techniques the CCP uses to achieve and maintain information dominance include the following:

Propaganda:

The Chinese Communists have a panoply of official outlets that push what is literally the "Party line" to the people of China and to audiences worldwide. According to Professor Kerry Gershaneck,[218] the author of *Political Warfare: Strategies for Combating China's Plan to "Win without Fighting"*[219] and *Media Warfare: Taiwan's Battle for the Cognitive Domain*[220]:

The People's Republic of China has invested a massive amount of money and resources into building a just overwhelming… some might say, a very large apparatus worldwide to wage what we call "media warfare." The goals of media warfare are pretty much the goals of all other political warfare: generate support at home, nationalize the Chinese people, make sure they're obedient. Part of political warfare has to do with violence and brutal repression: oppress them, beat them, send them to concentration camps, kill them if they don't comply internally. And then, abroad as well, generate support and destroy [the CCP's] critics, weaken our will to fight, create divisions amongst us.

Strategies that [the CCP is pursuing include]: saturate the information space; dominate the airwaves; dominate

*print media online; and social media warfare. They either
own or control the content delivery systems. That's the news
organizations, the WeChat, the taking over [and] putting
people inside our social media platforms.*

Mr. Weingarten describes a factor that contributes powerfully to the sort of control the CCP exercises over America's media—even in cases where outright ownership is not operating[221]:

*The media, of course, reflects the very same views as those at the
top of it, led in part by the idea, the belief—it's become a self-
fulfilling prophecy in some respects—that China will eclipse
us and that [we] ought to accommodate that eclipse through
integration, through "engagement." And ultimately, as we found
out, our relations with the Chinese Communist Party have
made the U.S. more like Communist China than Communist
China has become like the U.S.*

And, Ben Weingarten offers a specific example of this sort of CCP cooption of the Western media in practice in connection with China's COVID cover story:

*The Chinese Communist Party wanted to decouple the
pandemic from the CCP, and turning the attention to the
purported racism, bigotry, xenophobia in America was a
perfect narrative. CCP mouthpieces parroted that and talked
about America's problem with anti-Asian sentiment. Our
media claimed that it was a MAGA anti-Asian sentiment,
which is belied by anecdotal accounts and the numbers as well.*

*But it's worth noting that the reportage of numbers of this
"mass" of anti-Asian sentiment and rising hate crimes in this
country was largely driven by progressive groups, including
Asian identity-politics-focused progressive groups, who were
parroted in Chinese Communist Party media. You could
probably find links between those organizations and the CCP
or their front groups as well.*

Within China, the impact of this sort of indoctrination is reinforced by the so-called "Great Firewall," an electronic barrier to alternative sources of truthful information. In the event this Firewall is breached, the CCP uses its Social Credit System to monitor any content that is somehow taken aboard via traditional and social media or other communications platforms (e.g., phone calls, text messages, emails or even outdoors conversations monitored by the regime's ubiquitous surveillance cameras). Consumption of such unauthorized, if not actually illicit, information—let alone, its further dissemination—can *and does* result in harsh penalties.

In the United States, the impact of Chinese propaganda is enhanced by its paid placement in American media outlets in the form of "advertising supplements"[222] that largely appear indistinguishable from the rest of what is published by newspapers like the *New York Times* and the *Washington Post*. As such outlets confront ever more intense financial difficulties, the importance of the cash-infusions from Beijing appears to be influencing the papers' *own* reporting, as does pressure on their China-based correspondents to conform to the CCP's wishes.

Needless to say, the Chinese Communists would never allow the U.S. government or American media similar latitude to inseminate information favorable to this country or hostile to China inside the People's Republic.

Another battlespace in the CCP's information warfare is our culture from which, as Andrew Breitbart brilliantly noted, "politics is downstream." Mr. Gershaneck points to the Chinese censors operating in Hollywood, and, for that matter in Bollywood in India[223]: "They walk in and say, 'You ought to release your movie in China and make lots of money. You do exactly what we say to do with your script, and you carry the narratives that we want you to convey in the movie.'"

At the same time, the CCP has done with America's entertainment sector what they have done with U.S. businesses, in general, and our industrial base, in particular (see Charges 5 and 6), namely: buy up what they can (notably, studios and relevant technology firms); extract the requisite know-how needed to replicate and decisively compete with American producers (in this case, of films); then, dominate the market, hollowing out, if not destroying, U.S. rivals.

Today, China is increasingly generating movies for its market and sharply restricting the numbers of U.S. ones allowed to run in the PRC's immense numbers of theaters. The few made-in-America movies that make the cut these days for distribution in Communist China do not feature, let alone celebrate, this country, its strengths or freedoms.

Benjamin Weingarten brilliantly summarized the phenomenon of the CCP's elite capture in America's media and cultural institutions: "The Globalist project ought to be seen...as a *China First* project. To the extent our media is a supporter of that project...it would make sense that they would be China First in their outlook."

TikTok:

The CCP also uses an immensely popular application called TikTok to propagandize Americans, especially younger ones. It is, therefore, no accident that many in that age cohort believe, for example, that: their country is systematically racist; China had nothing to do with the pandemic that has killed more than a million of us; and socialism is a preferable form of governance. All of these are messages conveyed, often subliminally, via TikTok.

Brigadier General Robert Spalding, U.S. Air Force (Ret.) is a Mandarin-speaking former U.S. defense attaché in China and National Security Council strategist, a high-tech entrepreneur and author of *Stealth War: How China Took Over While America's Elites Slept*[224] and *War Without Rules: China's Playbook for Global Domination*.[225] He notes about the CCP's weaponization of TikTok[226]:

> *TikTok...mixes in China's dominance in artificial intelligence, along with the mass collection of data on individuals from free countries. The content that is pushed on TikTok in the free societies [is different from] what's pushed in China. So, the number one trending topic on TikTok in China is the idea that you want to become an astronaut....[By contrast,] in the West, the number one topic is how to become a social media influencer.*
>
> *The messages that are pushed on TikTok are used to convince people that China's model is better than the United States'. You can find Chinese propaganda that is verbatim the same text being read as scripts for different videos produced by different influencers in different locations and aimed at different audiences. So, not only are they advancing this idea of watching*

videos that don't contribute at all to the social good, but they're also influencing them to support principles that the Chinese Communist Party supports.

In other words, the CCP fully understands the power of this platform. It strictly limits Chinese kids' access to their version of the TikTok platform, Doyin. And, even then, they receive very different content than their peers in this country, namely videos promoting not only patriotism towards their motherland, but a life of hard work and achievement—a far cry from the self-indulgent narcissism, dissing of the United States and inducement to lassitude that is the steady diet of U.S. users.

Worse yet, such messaging is assiduously intensified by the sophisticated algorithms the TikTok app uses to make the silly dance micro-videos and other tripe served up by the platform as addictive as possible. The object is to ensure that both its subliminal and overt anti-U.S., pro-CCP propaganda are internalized by the app's American users to the maximum extent possible.

Joe Allen, an expert in transhumanism and other means of manipulating and enslaving homo sapiens, describes this attribute of TikTok as follows[227]:

> *The element of surveillance and the element of psychological manipulation really are the primary dangers of an app like TikTok, its addictive nature. It basically glues the mind to that digital environment and in the process is able to glean all of this information about users not only from the content that they view, but much more direct information such as their identity, their location. . . .*
>
> *You get the users addicted, the algorithm learns the user's preferences, and then the algorithm feeds that user the sorts of material that the person wants, but also the sorts of material that the corporation itself wants and the idea of social contagion. . . . People can be influenced en masse, their psychology can be influenced en masse, and maybe even change to the extent that they would accept something like a transgender ideology, or accept the sort of mass suppression we saw during the pandemic.*

Economist and expert on totalitarianism Connie Elliott points out this combination of addictiveness and subversive messaging amounts to a powerfully destructive weapon in the hands of our mortal enemy[228]: "How does one cause the revolution? One has to alienate the children from a society. You can't overthrow a society while children have hope, while families have hope, while kids believe that there's something good in what they were raised with and want to carry that onto tomorrow."

As retired Army Colonel John Mills, a specialist in psychological and cyberwarfare makes plain, the Chinese Communists' fearsome Ministry of State Security (MSS) is the driving force behind such manipulation of our children. Thanks to TikTok's ability to turn on a cell phone's camera and microphones without the knowledge of the owner, the app and its masters in China can collect untold amounts of personal data and other proprietary information (including your DNA), to the detriment not only of the user, but possibly the national security, as well. According to Mills[229]:

> You have to look at TikTok as the digital vanguard of Chinese civil-military fusion. That's what it's all about. If you do business in China, through the bylaws of the Chinese Communist Party apparatus, you essentially become an extension of the state, and that includes the state intelligence, the MSS, the Ministry of State Security. [TikTok is] essentially the big data analytics vanguard of the MSS, in a nice pretty package disguised as social media.

> They're collecting all aspects of us, all of our viewing activities. If you authenticate your phone, if you sign up for TikTok, you are granting permission for the MSS to intrude into your mobile device, whether it be a cell phone, a laptop, an iPad. You are essentially giving permission for the MSS to know everything about you and implant nefarious things so they can monitor your activity.

> There's a good chance everyone in the audience has a digital twin that is being developed by the CCP, massaged over time to higher and higher degrees of refinement, so they know everything about us. TikTok is the vanguard of that digital twin.

Joe Allen adds ominously[230]: "...All of this [data] is being aggregated into a digital twin, most importantly, a sort of *society of digital twins*. This is a way to model the internal psychology of individuals and the sociological landscape of any given society."

For all these reasons, President Trump contemplated banning the TikTok app[231] in the United States. While some states and federal agencies have prohibited it from operating on official phones, many tens of millions of American users continue to be subject to this all-too- seductive and diabolically problematic app.

General Spalding explains that, "The reason we don't ban WeChat and TikTok in the United States is the corporate lobby in Washington, D.C., both in Congress and the administration. We have to break through this gridlock in Washington. We have to break through the influence of the Chinese Communist Party on our corporate lobby."[232]

Robert Spalding reverts to the basic proposition that should, at a minimum, govern in U.S.-Chinese dealings:

> *No reciprocity between Chinese social media platforms and American social media platforms within China is an issue that should be covered under most favored nation trading status.... For example, China just recently said that no World of Warcraft games can be played in China anymore. But games from Tencent, a Chinese company, and apps like WeChat or Alibaba are freely available in the West. From a reciprocity standpoint, just in terms of the free market, if Twitter, Facebook and other social media platforms aren't available in China, then it seems logical that platforms like TikTok and WeChat should not be available in the United States.*

Even if we enjoyed reciprocal access for relatively benign U.S. apps in China, however, as Connie Elliott notes, do we really want an app with TikTok's characteristics to operate here?[233]

> *When you're in a situation in a user environment where you can see that training data are harvested on you, that algorithms are programmed based on that, that content is created or fed to you based on that algorithm and that your attention is fixated on it, or that your preference is based on the material you've seen*

only to repeat, then you know that you are in a system that is designed to bend your capacity to exercise free and unfettered choice. And we have to ask ourselves, is this the environment we want to live in, that we want our children to be interacting with?

The answer, of course, must be "No."

Confucius Influence Operations:

Yet another vehicle the CCP uses for propagandizing, indoctrinating and perhaps recruiting and elite-capturing young Americans is a Trojan horse operating in U.S. academia under the guise of language and cultural training programs best known as "Confucius Institutes" (CIs) and "Confucius Classrooms."

Confucius Institutes have, until recently, been operating on some 118 U.S. public and private college and university campuses. Under contracts that provide PRC funding for these programs to American schools, the CCP is entitled to engage in not just the CIs' stated purpose—namely, Mandarin training and promotion of Chinese culture. They can also dictate, or at least influence, decisions concerning: which faculty members are assigned to teach about China; their curricula; and even who is invited to speak to students about matters of interest to the CCP.

In addition, as the Association of American Scholars' specialist on Confucius operations, Dr. Ian Oxnevad, points out[234]:

> *One of the big problems with Confucius Institutes is that they would bring Chinese government policy into the classroom, as well as shaping perceptions about China and China's role in the world. You would have things like censorship. You have many cases of purported economic espionage involving Confucius Institutes. You have the surveillance of Chinese dissidents, other critics of China, as well as just the theft of intellectual property and other nefarious deeds.*

Dr. Oxnevad's organization led a much-needed, laudable and concerted effort to shut down the Confucius operations with its highly acclaimed reports, *Outsourced to China* (2017)[235] and *After Confucius Institutes: China's Enduring Influence on American Higher Education* (2022).[236] Here is his description of what happened[237]:

> When the pressure started to come on in 2019 to curtail [the
> CCP's Confucius operations], not just the U.S., but India,
> Europe, Australia and other countries have sought to close these
> institutes, as well. Many institutes "closed" but were replaced by
> something else. They either went through a rebranding process
> where the Confucius Institute was rebranded as another sort
> of program, while the relationship between universities in both
> countries was kept alive or even deepened.

The problem posed in this country by the CCP's academic influence
operations is not confined to higher education. Confucius Classrooms
allow the Chinese to penetrate schools serving younger American
students, thus, enabling the CCP to begin indoctrinating our children
at earlier and even more impressionable ages. Dr. Oxnevad observes:
"You would think that among all of the chatter about education reform,
Confucius Classrooms would at least pop up on the radar screen. But
unfortunately, it's not. And if you don't have sovereignty in your own
educational system, you don't really have sovereignty at all."

Anti-Communist freedom-fighter Trevor Loudon summarizes
the dangers posed by these CCP penetrations of America's academy as
follows[238]:

> [The Chinese Communists] have bought both sides of the aisle,
> and they are doing it through the Confucius Institutes, through
> business, etc. They are training the next leaders of business, new
> political leaders. They are the ones going on the trips to China.
> They are the ones learning Mandarin and being indoctrinated
> to take a soft approach to the CCP. ....I think it's about as critical
> as you can get. Having Confucius Institutes in the country right
> now is like having the Nazi youth set up branches all around
> America in 1938.

Naturally, if there were a corresponding, officially sponsored
American influence operation, it would not be allowed to engage in
reciprocal activities in China.

The CCP's United Fronts in America:

The Chinese Communist Party has a United Front Work Department dedicated to conducting information and influence operations in foreign countries and most especially the United States. It cultivates ties with think tanks and non-governmental organizations willing to accept funding, all-expenses-paid trips to China and similar benefits in exchange for helping the CCP develop relationships with governors, legislators, the media, business leaders and others targeted for Beijing's elite capture.

A preeminent social scientist who has long specialized on China's internal crimes against humanity and external threats to the rest of us, Steven Mosher, puts these operations in an historical context[239]:

> *I think it's interesting to look at the parallels between the approach that the Chinese Communist Party is using today and the approach that it used to take power in China, because there is a precise and exact parallel between the two. After all, Mao Tse-tung said that the Chinese Communist Party has three magic weapons: It has propaganda. It has United Front tactics, which include influence operations. And, of course, it has the People's Liberation Army. And they prefer to use [them] in that order. Propaganda to soften the minds and win the hearts of the people. United Front tactics [and] influence operations to weaken any elite opposition to their takeover. And finally, the People's Liberation Army marches in.*

While innumerable examples could be cited of United Front tactics at work in America, one of the Work Department's most successful influence operations here came to light in connection with the nomination in 2021 of the president of one CCP-allied U.S. think tank, the Carnegie Endowment for International Peace's William Burns, to become President Biden's Central Intelligence Agency director.[240] Mr. Burns was asked under oath by Senator Marco Rubio about the Carnegie Endowment's long history of collaborating with CCP influence operations. And the nominee lied.[241]

A former senior Foreign Service Officer, Deputy Secretary of State and Ambassador, William Burns testified that, when he joined the Endowment, he had been concerned about its programs with Chinese influence operators and promptly acted to shut them down. In fact, to the contrary, he continued *and expanded* them—even going so far as to place on his organization's Board of Directors a wealthy Chinese businessman active for many years in promoting the Communist Party's interests.

Neither Sen. Rubio nor the Senate Select Committee on Intelligence held Amb. Burns to account for his perjury and he is today running our nation's premier intelligence agency. The utter lack of accountability in this egregious case has only served further to embolden the Biden team to appoint with impunity to senior posts numerous others compromised by China (see Charge 3).

Wolf-warrior Diplomacy:

The elevation of what has been called Xi Jinping's "Dream Team" to run the U.S. government is just one of the factors that has encouraged the CCP to engage in a particularly audacious form of influence operations. The Chinese Communists call it "Wolf Warrior" diplomacy. Its practitioners include Beijing's top Foreign Ministry and national security officials and its ambassadors to the United States and our key allies. Its signature trait is aggressiveness laced with open contempt, especially for their American counterparts and the country they represent.

Former Under Secretary of Defense for Policy Douglas Feith characterizes the Chinese diplomatic conduct this way[242]:

> The Chinese have invested heavily in their wolf diplomacy and their international influence operations. What they do is a combination of intimidation and corruption, coercion and cooptation, threats and inducements.
>
> The Chinese do not have a small set of reasonable, minor demands, the satisfaction of which by reasonable accommodation would make them law-abiding citizens of a sensible international order. The Chinese have very large ambitions to dominate their region, to dominate militarily even beyond their region, to push the United States effectively out of Asia, and to completely change the way the world works. And people who think that the Chinese threat can be eliminated or even seriously mitigated through small measures of appeasement are misconstruing the nature and ambitions of the Chinese government.

Former Assistant Secretary of State Robert Charles puts a fine point on the gravity of the mistake involved in such efforts at accommodation of the CCP[243]:

> Weakness invites pushing the envelope, trying to see how far they can go. The charm offensive is over. It was for quite a while the notion that they could either try to charm Americans, essentially anesthetize us diplomatically so that we paid no attention to what was happening behind the curtain, or they simply denied things....The needle has moved over and there's now aggression in the vocabulary. And that is exactly because of [our] weakness.

Former Under Secretary of State Robert Joseph draws upon his personal experience with Wolf Warrior and other Chinese emissaries to underscore the effect our weakness has on their behavior[244]:

> Just a word on my interactions with Chinese diplomats over the course of many years and likely hundreds of conversations. It's clear that these emissaries are little more than barbarian-handlers and propagandists with no authority other than to repeat ad nauseam the talking points that are supplied by the Power Ministries and the party leadership in Beijing. So, when the Chinese ambassador is either gracious or, as we've seen more recently, haranguing and even threatening us, it's on the orders of those in Beijing who are orchestrating the war against us.
>
> In my experience, when we have not responded forcefully to threats and other forms of intimidation in the diplomatic channels, we have always paid a high price because weakness is sensed by the Chinese leadership and exploited.

As noted previously, proof of this insight was much in evidence in the Biden Administration's first face-to-face meeting between top U.S. officials and their counterparts in Alaska in March 2021.[245] As noted above, neither Secretary of State Antony Blinken nor National Security Advisor Jake Sullivan responded forcefully to the Chinese interlocutors' vociferous public attacks, let alone assertively denounced the CCP's record.

As the recent instance of Beijing's balloon belligerence[246] demonstrated anew, U.S. officials' supine behavior is hugely counterproductive. Perceived appeasement lends itself to two predictable repercussions—both contrary to U.S. interests: 1) The Chinese are further emboldened and reinforced in their conviction that the United States lacks the wherewithal to resist China's "rise." And 2) other nations have been encouraged to pursue a separate peace with the CCP.

Team Biden's Alaska debacle, followed by his humiliating defeat and surrender in Afghanistan, has only further catalyzed these twin phenomena. It also has compounded the demoralization of Americans, a central purpose of the Chinese Communists' information and influence operations.

Former Deputy National Security Advisor Matthew Pottinger, a fluent Mandarin-speaking former journalist in China, observes[247]:

> It's absolutely imperative we respond to that wolf warrior diplomacy. Sometimes responding can be done in a uniquely American way, by poking fun [at] some of the absurd statements that we're hearing Chinese diplomats, so-called diplomats, make on our shores. I think a lot of what China is doing is backfiring. But we need to call it out.
>
> American diplomacy is at its best when it's really plain spoken, when it's in the language of the American people. It doesn't mean bitter or intemperate, but calling things out in a plain-spoken way, not in diplomat[ese]. It means explaining what the purpose of China's rhetoric is when it crosses these lines, pointing out that it's designed to intimidate, but that we, like our friends and allies, are not going to be intimidated.

The CCP's Ethnic Fifth Column:

Another key audience for the Chinese Communists' information operations via propaganda, explicit directions and demands for submission is the worldwide diaspora of ethnic Chinese, in particular inside the United States. As China expert Gordon G. Chang has warned[248]:

> *At the end of July [2020], Chinese ruler Xi Jinping gave a landmark speech to the Communist Party's United Front Work conference in Beijing. In that speech, he called upon Communist Party cadres to unite Chinese people around the world in support of the Chinese state. So, in effect, he wanted to mobilize ethnic Chinese to be CCP agents.*
>
> *The Communist Party rejects the notion that ethnic Chinese, whether they were citizens of China and then left, or whether they were never citizens of China, can be loyal to any country other than China. So, in their view, there is no escape from ethnicity.*
>
> *The Communist Party is making overtly racial-based appeals. China's regime asks, cajoles, threatens and intimidates ethnic Chinese around the world to commit espionage and other crimes for the People's Republic. And as we know from successful prosecutions and guilty pleas from ethnic Chinese, they're quite successful in our country in doing that.*
>
> *We have to understand that the overwhelming majority of people of ethnic Chinese origin in our country are loyal to the United States. That's especially true of people who have escaped Chinese Communism. They know what is at stake.*
>
> *Xi Jinping right now is trying to create a Fifth Column of ethnic Chinese that are directed to destroy the country that we call home. The United States of America, our home, is at peril, [it] is under attack by the People's Republic of China. And we, Chinese Americans and other Americans have got to understand that and respond immediately.*

It is no secret that the federal agency that is principally charged with countering hostile intelligence operations inside the United States, the FBI, is hopelessly overwhelmed in doing just the task of monitoring and countering even a fraction of the more than 300,000 Chinese students currently studying in this country.[249] That would be the case if every FBI agent in the country were assigned to this mission.

Unfortunately, matters are made considerably worse by the reality that there are millions of *other* Chinese nationals and their progeny here, at least some of whom warrant rigorous counterintelligence surveillance. But the vast majority are not monitored at all. And the Biden administration actually ordered the FBI last year to shutter[250] one of its main efforts with respect to such monitoring—the woefully small and inadequately funded "China Initiative"[251]—out of concerns that its investigations would be seen as xenophobic and racist towards ethnic Chinese in the United States.

Just how serious a problem this reality has become can be sensed from this admonition by retired Air Force Colonel and former General Counsel to the Senate Intelligence Committee, Daniel Gallington[252]:

> In order [for a Chinese person] to come to the United States and for that matter, in order to travel outside of China, you have to get approval for whatever you're going to do [from] the central government—which implicitly includes tasking and cooperation. How the Chinese are intimidating their nationals to get information or to return [to] them if they want [them] to, is nothing new. The Chinese have been doing this for 50 years and will continue to do it.

The danger posed by a CCP Fifth Column in the United States has been greatly exacerbated by Team Biden's further dissipation of the FBI's limited counterintelligence assets and capabilities by directing the Bureau to give priority to pursuing Americans whom it slanders as "January 6th insurrectionists," "white supremacists," "domestic violent extremists" and "Christian nationalists."

The FBI has also been assigned the task of censoring anti-vaccine activists and other so-called "disinformers" for what amounts to their political opposition to the Biden regime. Some of the FBI's few Mandarin speakers and other counterintelligence professionals are deeply frustrated by being reassigned from contending with the CCP threat to what often amounts to the wholly unjustifiable surveilling, harassment and, in some cases, prosecution of patriotic Americans.

The predictable result is that, if and when the Chinese Communists launch a shooting war, we will likely not only find ourselves embroiled in devastating kinetic military conflict overseas, but we'll face a very serious threat to the homeland, namely from the CCP *inside our country.*

Overseas Police Service Centers:

The prospect that the already sizeable "enemy within" problem will be greatly magnified by the presence here of large numbers of Chinese Fifth Columnists was heightened by the opening in the United States of *at least one* so-called "Overseas Police Service Center." According to an analysis unveiled in September 2022 by a Madrid-based NGO called Safeguard Defenders, there are now scores of such CCP police outposts operating in nations worldwide[253]. While they are transparently assigned to monitor and otherwise "serve" Chinese expatriates, their real mission seems to be enforcing Xi's dictates with respect to their *serving the motherland* in whatever way is deemed necessary.

Former CIA spy Charles "Sam" Faddis described the contribution these installations make to the CCP's threat to the homelands of nations[254]:

> *There are at least 54 so-called overseas service centers being run by the Chinese government, scattered all over the globe. And these things have the purpose of facilitating the Chinese police, the Chinese authorities going out and putting hands on folks, Chinese citizens, and then compelling them to return to China. In the last year, something like 230,000 people—almost a quarter of a million Chinese—have been forced to return [to the PRC]. This is not extradition. This is not a legal proceeding. The Chinese are not working through local authorities. The Chinese are completely unilaterally reaching out and compelling people to return home no matter what they say.*
>
> *This is not an effort to go hunt down really bad people that have somehow fled abroad. This is an effort to target dissidents. No matter what verbiage they may use about persuasion or so forth, this is functionally kidnapping. What the [CCP's overseas police] do is grab a hold of these people, they bring them in, or they visit them at their homes and they lean on them.*
>
> *They bring you in and they put you on a video link with your grandmother who still lives in China. She's there sobbing and*

crying, and there are Chinese authorities in the room with her. She is completely at the mercy of this thuggish criminal enterprise, the CCP. And basically, either you're going to do what the Chinese authorities told you to do or grandma is going to face the consequences. There's nothing subtle about this. They don't beat around the bush. This is sort of the ultimate godfather making you an offer you can't refuse.

While the FBI reportedly raided and closed[255] that one facility in New York recently, it is unclear whether there are any other such sites still operating here and, if so, how many. Moreover, the Chinese Communists certainly have, *and use,* other means of exercising such fearsome control over the Chinese-American community.

Former Foreign Service Officer and Marine Colonel Grant Newsham describes some of the other elements of the PRC's coercive infrastructure this way[256]:

You have people in the Chinese embassies, consulates whose role is to intimidate and threaten the Chinese people living overseas. And they've been allowed to get away with this. Many of these Chinese people came to this country because they want to get away from these demons and here, we allow them to be intimidated. It's just like the mafia leaning on people. And this is something that we need to get a handle on really quickly.

The message is clear: *Do as you are told or something bad will happen to your relative.* The effect is surely not lost on more than the individual immediately subjected to this form of coercion. Others in the community are, thereby, placed on notice that their own loved ones could meet a similar fate.

The dire implications for our internal security cannot be lost on the rest of us, either. Former Force Reconnaissance Marine and FBI Special Agent John Guandolo characterizes this way the cost to *every* American and to our country arising from the Biden administration's record of willful blindness towards the CCP's New York police station even after its presence was made known publicly by Safeguard Defenders[257]:

Police stations and nodes for police activity by the Chinese Communists outside of China are being used to monitor Chinese citizens and potentially take action on them, which violates U.S. law, international law, all kinds of treaties. It's dangerous not only to our national security from a strategic standpoint. We are once again telling the Chinese we don't have any backbone to enforce U.S. law or even follow the standards of international norms. And that gives them the energy and the power and the desire to do more inside the United States. Because when we are weak, that opens us up to some real damage by our adversaries, including the Chinese.

Taken together, these nine Charges constitute a damning indictment of a) the Transnational Criminal Organization doing business as the Chinese Communist Party[258] and b) its crimes against its own people and its war crimes against ours. The costs of such crimes have been incalculably high. And, to date, the CCP has suffered no appreciable penalties, either for its mass destruction of China's own population and those of its Captive Nations or for its unrestricted warfare against ours.

The new House Select Committee on the Strategic Competition Between the United States and the Chinese Communist Party is the most promising vehicle at the moment for performing a rigorous assessment of these Charges and effectively prosecuting the case against the perpetrators—at least in the court of public opinion[259]. It is our profound hope that the Select Committee, the Congressional-Executive Commission on China and other House and Senate committees of jurisdiction will draw upon both the content of the Committee on the Present Danger: China's and related webinars[260] to date and take testimony from those whose participation in them contributed so powerfully to the generation of that content.

As a further contribution the situational awareness of the American people and to the work of their elected representatives, Part II of this book identifies twenty specific steps the United States should promptly take to: hold the Chinese Communist Party accountable; impose appropriate penalties; and protect our nation and people from past, present and future assaults by our mortal enemy, the CCP. Then, Part III describes several means by which such steps can translate into decisive action.

PART II

What Must We Do? Twenty Action Items to Protect America and Defeat the CCP

The following are illustrative of the sorts of steps that are, in light of the foregoing Charges against the Chinese Communist Party, now absolutely necessary. If fully implemented, they will mete out appropriate punishments for the CCP's criminal conduct. Even more importantly, they will help mitigate the damage done to date to our people and country by the Communist Chinese's unrestricted warfare against us—and enhance deterrence of the shooting war Xi Jinping seeks to inflict next.

1. Understand the threat

Before we can do anything material about the Chinese Communist Party's unrestricted warfare against the United States, we must identify and understand both the nature of its criminal conduct against us—past, present and prospective—and resolve to counter it and defeat the perpetrator.

This will require rigorous and comprehensive official investigations by the Congress, including ideally field hearings which will bring insights like those developed by the Committee on the Present Danger: China to the widest possible audience and afford opportunities for testimony to be taken by a representative sample of the many, many millions of us who have been harmed by the CCP's war crimes against America and other crimes against humanity.

2. Investigate Biden, his subordinates and others for "elite capture" by the CCP

It is not possible to say with certitude at present how much damage has been done to U.S. national security by the Chinese Communist Party's success in capturing America's business, financial, media, academic, cultural and political elites. But, given the extraordinary stakes involved, every effort must be made to assess the resulting negative effects as an essential precursor to mitigating them.

3. Remove from office/demand resignations of those compromised

It follows that, once individuals in government and other vital sectors of our nation are determined to have been suborned, subverted, recruited or otherwise compromised/controlled by the Chinese Communist Party, they must be removed from their respective roles. If necessary, they should be compelled to resign or be impeached. Where appropriate, they should be prosecuted for betraying our country.

4. Delegitimize the CCP

President Reagan demonstrated in his successful effort to defeat the last totalitarian Communist foe that sought America's destruction the importance of delegitimating the enemy. His famous characterization of the Soviet Union as the "Evil Empire" perfectly characterized our adversary, challenged its claim to power and emboldened those who yearned for freedom behind the Iron Curtain. The same must now be done with respect to the Chinese Communist Party.

For starters, the United States should officially designate to Chinese Communist Party as what it is: a Transnational Criminal Organization (TCO). As the evidence presented in this *Indictment* makes clear, such a designation is fully warranted on the basis of: the CCP's crimes against humanity; its enslavement of existing Captive Nations (East Turkistan, Tibet, Southern Mongolia and Hong Kong) and its hope to enslave many more through the Belt-and-Road initiative; and the war crimes against America arising from the unrestricted warfare to which we have been subjected for decades.

5. Adopt a war-footing

The Chinese Communist Party has patiently and assiduously put the people and nation it misrules on a war-footing. The United States has, to this point, taken very limited, if any, such steps. If we persist in leaving the Chinese Communists with decisive advantages in all those respects, we further encourage the belief that they can act with impunity, including militarily, against us.

6. Rebuild and replenish the U.S. military

It goes without saying that there can be no *real* war-footing if the United States' armed forces are unable to deter aggression against this country and/or unready to defeat such aggression if deterrence fails. To correct the grievous undermining of our armed services by the Biden administration, a number of corrective actions are required, including the following.

7. Disengage from China economically by, among other steps, weaning this country as soon as possible from the CCP's strategic supply chains

The distinct prospect (if not the virtual certitude) that the United States and its friends and allies will be attacked by Communist China moves the need to end our reliance on the CCP for critical commodities from a desirable, if difficult, objective to an *absolute necessity*. If we are to prevent an otherwise predictable economic and societal train-wreck, every effort must be made—including: tax incentives, encouraging patriotic investing instead of investments in our enemy, statutory and regulatory inducements and/or sanctions and public shaming—to promote onshoring. If necessary, in the short-run, diversification of foreign suppliers of such commodities should be promoted as long as they are not also dependent on Chinese sources or simply cut-outs for the CCP.

8. Cut off financing of any Chinese companies listed on U.S. exchanges or traded there

An even more immediate and cost-effective option for depriving the CCP of the underwriting that is enabling its unrestricted warfare against us would be to prevent Chinese companies from securing funding from U.S. capital markets. To do otherwise simply ensures that American investors will lose their shirts when China launches its kinetic war against us and our allies. If that were not disincentive enough for Wall Street mavens to stop putting their clients' funds at material risk with the CCP, another consideration might prove persuasive: By doing so, they are aiding and abetting our mortal enemy and, were the Party to be designated a Transnational Criminal Organization, accessories to its criminal conduct.

9. Allow no further U.S. purchases of Chinese sovereign bonds until the CCP pays investors for outstanding debts *all* those for which it is now responsible

In 1997, Communist China agreed to assume the responsibility for compensating British holders of gold-backed sovereign bonds issued early in the last century by the then-government of China. It did so as part of the negotiations that resulted in the surrender of Hong Kong by the United Kingdom to the PRC. The Chinese Communist Party has, however, adamantly refused to do the same for American holders of the same sovereign bonds.

Consequently, the U.S. government should prohibit further purchase and holding of Chinese-Communist-issued sovereign debt instruments at a minimum until the PRC has compensated American bond-holders of pre-Communist sovereign debt on terms no less favorable to those afforded those investors' British counterparts.

10. Bar the Federal Thrift Savings Plan from holding Chinese companies in its I-Fund or offering mutual funds that contain them via its Mutual Fund Window

For the foregoing reasons, the federal government's pension system, the Thrift Savings Plan (TSP) must not be a funding source for the Chinese Communist Party. That is especially the case insofar as the TSP's International Fund (I Fund) currently compels its participants to invest in 35 Chinese companies. Among them are corporations sanctioned by the U.S. government for human rights and/or national security reasons.

11. Shut down Confucius Institutes and Confucius Classrooms in the United States and replace them with *American* educational programs

Decisive action is required to shut down these influence operations masquerading as educational programs, once and for all. Instead of allowing the CCP to buy access to and influence with U.S. academic institutions, the federal government should, wherever possible in concert with state-level governments, do as was done in the Cold War with the Soviet Union—namely, mount its own national security-enhancing program for training about China's language and culture and otherwise equip Americans to understand and defeat the Chinese Communist Party.

12. Shut down any and all extraterritorial Chinese police operations in the United States

It is a national security threat, as well as a human rights affront, to have the Chinese Communist Party operating even a single so-called "Overseas Police Service Center" in this country, let alone possibly a multitude of them. At best, these are extraterritorial vehicles for surveilling, monitoring and controlling Chinese nationals, expatriates and their descendants in this country. At worst, they are instruments for compelling dissidents to return to horrible fates in China and coercing others in this country to serve as Fifth Columnists for the CCP. We need to assure that with the reported closure of the facility in New York City, there are no other such centers operating *anywhere* in the United States. We should also encourage and assist other countries in shutting those Overseas Chinese Police Service Centers operating on their soil.

13. Shutter United Front operations and the Chinese diplomatic operations running them

The Chinese Communist Party has long used its United Front Work Department to stand up, underwrite and otherwise work with influence operations in targeted countries and especially the United States. It is reckless, if not suicidal, to enable Chinese influence operatives to foster and collaborate with subversive organizations in America. Non-governmental, non-profit and other entities with demonstrable ties to the CCP must lose their tax-exempt status as a first step toward putting them out of business, lest they contribute materially to the take-down of our nation.

14. Ban TikTok and other national security-threatening apps

A growing number of influential public and private sector Americans are calling for the United States to ban TikTok, and with good reason: It is insane to enable the Chinese Communists to enjoy such unfettered access, especially to impressionable youths, when we know it is being exploited to: collect personal and possibly sensitive data; encourage indolence and anti-American attitudes; and promote pro-Chinese sentiment and conduct.

15. Prohibit Huawei and ZTE products and services, as well as DJI and other Chinese drones

The CCP's civil-military fusion agenda has resulted among other things in the proliferation of Chinese companies, products and services that are nominally marketed to civilian users for personal and commercial purposes. But, in practice, such things as Huawei and ZTE telecommunications equipment, software and services and DJI's hugely popular drones enable the Chinese Communists to penetrate and undermine the United States' and other nations' security and sovereignty. Every effort must be made to depict such products as *weapons* being wielded against this country as well as our partners and allies and, therefore, barred from use either here or by those with whom we wish to share intelligence and otherwise interoperate.

16. Ban CCP and cut-outs' purchase of farmland and food production companies

The absurdity of allowing the Chinese Communists to own and exploit our farmland and other real estate, especially in proximity to strategic assets, should be self-evident. The problem of potential Fifth Columnists here—particularly with some 300,000 Chinese nationals studying in the U.S., and untold numbers of others employed in this country—is acute enough without compounding it further by selling off American assets that will afford cover, proximity and opportunities to PLA, Ministry of State Security or other operatives to wage war against us *from within.*

17. Mandate a reworked Committee on Foreign Investment in the United States

A potential step towards precluding the reckless sale of strategic assets like farmland and other real estate in sensitive locations to Communist China is a retooled Committee on Foreign Investment in the United States (CFIUS). For that to be the case, however, there must be urgent structural reforms of that bureaucratic entity, starting with the removal of the Treasury Department, which reflexively favors foreign investment in this country, to be replaced with the relatively security-minded Departments of Commerce and Defense as its co-chairs.

18. Treat the Strategic Petroleum Reserve as the national security asset it is

End the disbursement of oil from the Strategic Petroleum Reserve (SPR) for any reason other than legitimate national security considerations. And, obviously, under no circumstances should oil from the SPR be sold to the Chinese Communists—especially when, to add insult to injury, they are making such purchases to increase *their own* emergency energy stockpiles.

19. Secure the Grid

All transformers, SKADA systems, computers, chips and other equipment manufactured in China and now literally "inside the wire" of the U.S. electric grid must be immediately: inventoried; examined for electronic trap-doors or other means of remotely controlling, disrupting and/or destroying those assets; and, wherever possible, swiftly removed from service in the U.S. electric grid. A small portion of the recently enacted $1.2 trillion infrastructure bill must be allocated to this and other measures to assure the resiliency of what is our most critical of critical infrastructures—the U.S. bulk power distribution system.

20. Insist on full reciprocity in any area not addressed above

If there remain elements of the Chinese Communist Party's activities in this country that are somehow determined to be in the United States' vital interest to continue, the decision to permit that to happen should be predicated on the principle of reciprocity. And, in the absence of reciprocal arrangements for U.S. government and/or private sector entities in China, any such CCP activities must be subject to the highest-level review, approval process, and oversight and treated as a rare exception to that rule.

PART III

How to Get the Action Items Done

Once a compelling indictment has been handed down in the court of public opinion and actions that will appropriately punish the Chinese Communist Party for its war crimes against us and its other crimes against humanity; mitigate the damage thus done to date; and/or prevent worse to come in the future, the question becomes: How will such actions be achieved?

The following are examples of the means by which that can happen:

A. Public Awareness Begets Public Engagement

Under present circumstances, in which the Chinese Communist Party has so successfully captured American elites, the only hope for materially changing the trajectory of "China's inevitable rise" and "America's inevitable decline" is for the people who stand to lose their country and freedoms to the CCP's unrestricted warfare to refuse to go there. That will require both their being exposed to the facts and equipped to translate their sentiments into action. Specifically, the public must be motivated to demand corrective measures. *The Indictment* is designed to facilitate each of these prerequisites.

B. Congressional Investigations

The primary focus of the sort of popular engagement *The Indictment* is intended to foster will be to press elected representatives—most especially the new House majority—to engage in unstinting investigations of: a) the pre-kinetic warfare in which the CCP has engaged against America for decades, and b) the help it has received in doing so from captured elites in this country.

The usefulness of such inquiries, however, may depend upon a resumption of the no-holds-barred fight that denied Kevin McCarthy the

House speakership until the fifteenth roll-call vote to ensure that he will neither bar nor restrict the investigators from following the evidence where it leads. In particular, he must support investigations and accountability concerning any compromise of legislators, *perhaps including some in his own Republican caucus,* and by donors tied to the Chinese Communists.

Every available panel of jurisdiction should be charged with exposing the ground truth that the CCP is at war with America, including: Armed Services, Intelligence, Judiciary, Oversight, Foreign Affairs, Ways and Means, the Select Committee on the Competition Between the United States and the Chinese Communist Party and the Congressional-Executive Commission on China. The webinars, books and other content drawn upon for *The Indictment* can and should be used to inform, structure and select witness and staff for these inquiries.

C. Congressional Reforms

In the face of the CCP's concerted, sustained and well-funded efforts to capture U.S. political (as well as other) elites, it is no longer tolerable to confer access to classified information on federal legislators simply by dint of the fact that they were elected to the House or the Senate.

Every member of Congress should be subjected to a security background check that examines, among other things, any associations with or funding received from corporate entities, organizations or individuals working with or on behalf of the Chinese Communist Party, to say nothing of any seeking the overthrow of our constitutional Republic. Such background checks must be conducted by veteran counter-intelligence professionals, not political appointees. Those who fail such vetting must be ineligible for Committees responsible for sensitive national security matters and access to classified information. Public notice should be given as to any failure to be cleared, and why.

D. Criminal Referrals

If warranted by the results of these investigations, the respective committees should refer to the Justice Department those deemed to have committed crimes on behalf of and/or otherwise to the benefit of the Chinese Communist Party. As congressional criminal referrals have been ignored by previous Justice Departments—and surely would be by *this one*, the principal benefit of formally voting out such recommendations would be to further heighten public awareness about, and channel the American people's anger concerning, the betrayals of our country by captured elites.

E. Impeachments and Other Vehicles for Accountability

What the U.S. House of Representatives *does have* the exclusive authority to do is to consider the impeachment of officeholders who it believes have violated the law, in the case of the president by committing "high crimes and misdemeanors." This option must be pursued with a view to removing from their present posts and responsibilities individuals determined by the relevant investigations to have been compromised by the Chinese Communist Party—and, by so doing, betrayed our country.

At present, this political corrective likely will not result in convictions by the Senate. But it can have the effect of illuminating misconduct that should be deemed disqualifying—and spotlight in their own right those who vote to acquit such individuals for formal and/or informal investigation.

Taken together, the facts marshalled in this Indictment, the recommended corrective actions proposed herein and the various vehicles for bringing them to bear can—if adopted promptly—offer patriotic Americans a chance to save our nation from the destruction the Chinese Communist Party has as its unwavering objective. We must not allow this opportunity to defeat our time's existential threat to freedom to slip from our grasp. Or, as Ronald Reagan warned, we will be reduced to "telling our children and our children's children what it was like in America when men were free."[1]

---

1   Ronald Reagan, *Encroaching Control*, Ronald Reagan Library, speech, (30 March 1961), https://www.reaganlibrary.gov/archives/audio/ronald-reagans-speech-phoenix-arizona-encroaching-control; https://archive.org/details/RonaldReagan-EncroachingControl

Participants in Webinars Relevant to the Indictment of the Chinese Communist Party[2]

Dr. Paul Alexander, PhD, COVID-19 Consultant Researcher in Evidence Based Medicine, Research Methodology, and Clinical Epidemiology

Joe Allen, Expert on Transhumanism and "the Bio-Digital Convergence"

Dr. Sanj Altan, PhD, President of Mongol-American Cultural Association

Dr. Greg Autry, PhD, Former White House Liaison to NASA; former NASA Chief Financial Officer-designate; co-author of *Death by China* and producer of a documentary film of the same name; and Clinical Professor of Space Leadership, Policy and Business at Arizona State University*

Abduweli Ayup, Linguist, survivor of the CCP concentration camps

Honorable Michele Bachmann, Former Member of Congress; former presidential candidate; Dean, Robertson School of Government, Regent University

Stephen K. Bannon, Host, *War Room Pandemic*; former Chief Strategist to the President; filmmaker, *In the Face of Evil*; freedom-fighter*

Kyle Bass, Chief Investment Officer, Hayman Capital; founder, Conservation Equity Management; driving force behind the Lone Star Infrastructure Protection Act*

Dr. Darren Beattie, PhD, Former White House speechwriter and policy aide; founder, Revolver.news

John Beaudoin, Sr., Bachelor of Science degree in Computer and Systems Engineering; an MBA in Management, and worked more than 30 years in the semiconductor research and development industry; COVID dataset forensic analysist on government abuse and corruption

---

2 The individuals whose brief, and generally partial, biographies are listed here were sponsored by: the Committee on the Present Danger: China; the CPDC's Stop Vaccine Passports Task Force; or its co-sponsor, the Center for Security Policy.

Todd Bensman, Former investigative journalist; former intelligence analyst, Texas Department of Public Safety; National Security Fellow, Center for Immigration Studies; author, *Overrun: How Joe Biden Unleashed the Greatest Border Crisis in U.S. History* and *America's Covert Border War: The Untold Story of the Nation's Battle to Prevent Jihadist Infiltration*

Ben Bergquam, Border Correspondent for Real America's Voice; Host, *Law and Border*

Lieutenant General Robert "Rod" Bishop, U.S. Air Force (Ret.), Former Commander, 3rd Air Force; Chairman of the Board, Stand Together Against Racism and Radicalism in the Services (STARRS)

Dr. Stephen Blank, PhD, Senior Fellow, Foreign Policy Research Institute; former Professor, Army War College; Author, *Light from the East: Russia's Quest for Great Power Status in Asia*

Lieutenant General William "Jerry" Boykin, U.S. Army (Retired): Former Deputy Under Secretary of Defense; former Commander, Delta Force*

Dr. Francis Boyle, PhD, professor of international law at the University of Illinois College of Law. He received his JD degree magna cum laude from Harvard Law School, and a PhD in Political Science from Harvard University. Professor Boyle served on the Board of Directors of Amnesty International

Trayce Bradford, Eagle Forum's National Issues on Human Trafficking and Policy Advisor for Freedoms Fund USA, Past President of Eagle Forum Texas, former candidate for Lieutenant Governor of Texas

Dr. Peter Breggin, MD, Acclaimed American Psychiatrist, Medical Health Watchdog and anti-corruption activist, Author of *COVID-19 and the Global Predators: We are the Prey*

Colonel Mark Cancian, U.S. Marine Corps Reserves (Ret.); combat veteran; former Chief of the Force Structure and Investment Division, Office and Management and Budget; former official, Office of the Secretary of Defense; former head of research, Harvard Kennedy School

Joel Caplan, Investor in a Chinese NASDAC-listed corporation who was defrauded out of millions of dollars in capital and has been unable to collect in judgments

Nathan Carson, Vice President, Chemical Dynamics, Inc., expert on food security, fertilizer industry and supply chain management

Gordon G. Chang, Esq., Senior Fellow, Gatestone Institute; columnist, *Newsweek*; author, *The Coming Collapse of China*

Chris Chappell, Host, "China Uncensored"

Honorable Robert Charles, Esq., Former Assistant Secretary of State for Narcotics and Law Enforcement Affairs; former U.S. Navy intelligence officer; former White House congressional counsel; author, *Eagles and Evergreens*; and Principal, The Charles Group*

Ambassador/Dr. Henry Cooper, PhD, Former Air Force officer; former Deputy Assistant Secretary of the Air Force; former Assistant Director of the Arms Control and Disarmament Agency; former U.S. Ambassador to the U.S.-Soviet Defense and Space Talks; former Director, Strategic Defense Organization; Chairman of the Board of Directors, High Frontier*

Lance Crayon, Investigative journalist; writer; documentary filmmaker; former senior news editor of a leading Chinese Communist propaganda instrument, *Global Times*

Secretary Seth Cropsey, Former Deputy Under Secretary of the Navy; former Assistant to the Secretary of Defense; Senior Fellow and Director, American Seapower Program, Hudson Institute; author, *Mayday: The Decline of American Naval Supremacy* and *Seablindness: How Political Neglect is Choking American Seapower and What to do About It*

Honorable Kenneth Cuccinelli, Former Acting Secretary and Deputy Secretary of Homeland Security; former Director, U.S. Customs and Border Enforcement; former Attorney General of Virginia; former Virginia State Senator; Senior Fellow, Center for Renewing America

Ambassador Kelley Currie, Former Ambassador-at-Large for Global Women's Issues; former U.S. Representative to the U.N. Economic and Social Council; former Director, State Department Office of Global Criminal Justice

Honorable Kenneth DeGraffenreid, Captain, U.S. Navy (Retired); former Special Assistant to the President for Intelligence; former Deputy U.S. Counter-Intelligence Executive*

Honorable/Lieutenant Colonel Chuck DeVore, U.S. Army Reserves (Ret.); former member, California State Assembly; Chief National

Initiatives Officer, Texas Public Policy Institute; author,

Elaine Donnelly, Founder and President, Center for Military Readiness; former member, Defense Advisory Committee on Women in the Services; former member, Presidential Commission on the Assignment of Women in the Armed Forces

Allan Dos Santos, International political journalist; founder of *Terça Livre*

Christine Douglass-Williams, International award-winning journalist; a former Director of the Canadian Race Relations Foundation; daily writer, Jihad Watch; Contributing Editor, Frontpage Magazine; author of *The Challenge of Modernizing Islam*

Dr. Henry Ealy, DNM, Founder of the Energetic Health Institute; host of Energetic Health Radio

Myron Ebell, Director for Energy and Environment, Competitive Enterprise Institute; Chairman, Cooler Heads Coalition; and former leader of the Trump Presidential Transition's agency action team, Environmental Protection Agency

Nicholas Eftimiades, Former career official with the U.S. Central Intelligence Agency, the Department of State and Defense Intelligence Agency; Senior Fellow, Atlantic Council; creator of an online course entitled, *Chinese Intelligence: Operations and Tactics*

Honorable Tsakhiagiin Elbegdorj, Prime Minister (1998, 2004-2006) and President (2009-2017) of Mongolia

Sheriff Bill Elder, El Paso County Sheriff (Ret.)

Connie Elliott, Economist; Subject Matter Expert on totalitarianism

Jonathan Emord, Esq. JD, Former Federal Communications Commission attorney; constitutional attorney and litigator; author, *The Authoritarians: Their Assault on Individual Liberty, the Constitution, and Free Enterprise from the 19th Century to the Present*; candidate for U.S. Senate from Virginia

Treniss Evans, Founder, CondemnedUSA.com; January 6th defendant; star of documentary *Bloody Hill: The Seven Deadly Sins of January 6th*

Charles "Sam" Faddis, Former career CIA Clandestine Service operations officer; author, *Beyond Repair: The Decline and Fall of the CIA;*

and principal, AND Magazine on Substack*

Captain James Fanell, USN (Ret.): Former Chief of Intelligence and Information Operations, U.S. Pacific Fleet*

Honorable Douglas Feith, Esq., Former Under Secretary of Defense for Policy; former Deputy Assistant Secretary of Defense for Negotiations Policy; author, *War and Decision: Inside the Pentagon at the Dawn of the War on Terrorism*; Senior Fellow, Hudson Institute

Richard Fisher, Senior Fellow for Asia, International Assessment and Strategy Center; and author, *China's Military Modernization: Building for Global and Regional Reach*

Enes Kanter Freedom, International and NBA basketball star; Human Rights Advocate; and freedom-fighter

Kevin Freeman, CFA, Host of "Economic War Room with Kevin Freeman"; President, National Security Investment Consultants Institute; author, "Secret Weapon: *How Economic Terrorism Brought Down the U.S. Stock Market and How It Can Happen Again, Game Plan: How to Protect Yourself from the Coming Cyber-Economic Attack* and *According to Plan: The Elites' Secret Plan to Sabotage America*

Frank J. Gaffney, Executive chairman for the Center for Security Policy; Real America's Voice host of *Securing America with Frank Gaffney*; and Vice Chairman, Committee on the Present Danger: China; Co-Chairman, Stop Vaccine Passports Task Force; lead author, *War-Footing: Ten Steps America Must Take to Prevail in the War for the Free World*

Dr. Francesco Gallietti, PhD, Co-founder and CEO, Policy Sonar; International Geostrategic Consultant

Colonel Dan Gallington, USAF (Ret.), former Deputy Counsel for Intelligence Policy at the Justice Department; former bi-partisan General Counsel for the Senate Intelligence Committee; former Deputy Assistant Secretary of Defense for Territorial Security*

Honorable Heidi Ganahl, Member, University of Colorado Board of Regents (January 11, 2017 – January 5, 2023); former Republican nominee for governor of Colorado

Charles Gerow, Vice Chairman of the Conservative Political Action Conference and the American Conservative Union; CEO of Quantum

Communications; and former candidate for governor of Pennsylvania

Professor Kerry Gershaneck, Visiting Scholar at National Chengchi University in Taiwan and other universities in Asia; former strategic planner and spokesman for the Office of the Secretary of Defense; author, *Political Warfare: Strategies for Combating China's Plan to "Win without Fighting"* and *Media Warfare: Taiwan's Battle for the Cognitive Domain*

Kalbinur Gheni, Sister of a detainee in a Chinese Communist Party concentration camp for Uighurs

Rosemary Gibson, Senior Advisor, The Hastings Center; co-author, *China Rx: Exposing the Risk of America's Dependence on China for Medicine**

Dr. G. Weldon Gilcrease, MD, Associate Professor, Oncology Division, University of Utah School of Medicine; a Huntsman Cancer Institute investigator

Honorable Louie Gohmert, Esq., nine-term Member of Congress from Texas (January 3, 2005 – January 3, 2023); former Texas District Judge; and Chief Justice of the Texas 12th Circuit Court of Appeals; former U.S. Army officer

Dr. Sasha Gong, PhD, Former political prisoner in Communist China; former China Branch Chief, Voice of America; author of *Born American: A Chinese Woman's Dream of Freedom*; and documentary filmmaker*

Victor González, Member, Spain's Congress of Deputies; spokesperson for the Chairman of the Congress of Deputies' Foreign Affairs Committee

Dr. Evelyn Griffin, MD, physician double-Board Certified in Ostetrics and Gynecology

John Guandolo, Combat veteran U.S. Marine Force Reconnaissance Officer; former FBI Special Agent and Investigator, Counterterrorism Division; founder, Understanding the Threat

Honorable Bob Hall, Texas State Senator; and former U.S. Air Force officer

Captain Bill Hamblet, U.S. Navy (Ret.), Editor-in-Chief, U.S. Naval Institute *Proceedings*

Colonel Derek Harvey, U.S. Army (Ret.), former Senior Analyst for Iraq, Joint Staff Directorate for Intelligence; former Chief, Commander's Assessments and Initiatives Group, Iraq; former Professional Staff Member, House Permanent Select Committee on Intelligence; former

National Security Council staff member; and Commissioner, Maryland's Washington County Commission

Dr. Steven Hatfill, MD, MSc, MSc, MMeD, Former Senior Medical Advisor to the Executive Office of the President; Member Team B III; author, *Three Seconds to Midnight,* co-author of *The CCP is at War with America**

Edward Haugland, Veteran federal Senior Executive in Intelligence Community and other national security agencies; CEO of Edward Haugland LLC

Will Hild, President, *Consumer's Research*

Ambassador Pete Hoekstra, Former Member of Congress and Chairman of the House Intelligence Committee; former U.S. Ambassador to the Netherlands*

Leo Hohmann, Veteran investigative reporter; author, *Stealth Invasion;* contributor to: *FrontPage Magazine, LifeSite News, Zero Hedge* and *The Gateway Pundit*

The Right Reverend Stanley Hotay, Anglican Bishop of the Mount Kilimanjaro Diocese in Tanzania

Joseph Humire, Marine combat veteran; Executive Director, Center for a Secure Free Society; author of *Iran's Strategic Penetration of Latin America*

Elfidar Iltebir, President, Uyghur American Association (UAA)

Reverand Kevin Jessip, President, Global Strategic Alliance; and President, the Return International*

Brad Johnson, Former Senior Operations Officer and Chief of Station, Central Intelligence Agency; and founder and President, Americans for Intelligence Reform*

Ambassador Robert Joseph, Former Under Secretary of State for Arms Control and International Security; former U.S. Ambassador to the Standing Consultative Commission; former Special Envoy for Nuclear Non-proliferation; and Senior Scholar, National Institute for Public Policy*

Dr. Phillip Karber, PhD, Marine Corps veteran; longtime public servant in the national security arena; former senior defense industry executive; former professor at Georgetown University, the National War College, and other academic institutions*

Ross Kennedy, Founder, Fortis Analysis; a long-time executive and consultant in the food production sector

Brian Kennedy, Chairman, Committee on the Present Danger: China; President of American Strategy Group; former President, Claremont Institute*

Dr. Aaron Kheriaty, MD, Former Professor of Psychiatry at University of California Irvine (UCI) School of Medicine and Director of the Medical Ethics Program at UCI Health; author, *The New Abnormal: The Rise of the Biomedical Security State*; Fellow and Director of the Program in Bioethics and American Democracy at the Ethics and Public Policy Center; Senior Scholar at the Brownstone Institute

Se Hoon Kim, Director of the Captive Nations Coalition of the Committee on the Present Danger: China*

Steve Kirsch, Founder, Covid-19 Early Treatment Fund (CETF); inventor and entrepreneur; Silicon Valley philanthropist; founder, Vaccine Safety Research Foundation (VSRF)

Dr. Pierre Kory, MD, Pulmonary and Critical Care Specialist; President and Chief Medical Officer, Front Line Critical Care Alliance.

Dr. Matthew Kroenig, PhD, Former official in the Office of the Secretary of Defense; former member, Central Intelligence Agency's Strategic Assessments Group; Director of Studies, Atlantic Council and Acting Director of the Council's Scowcroft Center for Strategy and Security; author, *The Return of Great Power Rivalry*

Shali Kumar, Inventor; entrepreneur; industrialist; Chairman and CEO of AVG Advanced Technology*

Lieutenant General Stephen Kwast, U.S. Air Force (Ret.), Former Commander, Air Education and Training Command; former Commander and President, Air University; and combat command pilot

Sasha Latypova, Ex-pharma/biotech executive with 25 years of experience working for 60+ pharma companies worldwide, specializing in clinical trials, clinical technologies and regulatory approvals, including with the FDA.

Dede Laugesen, Executive Secretary, Committee on the Present Danger: China; and Executive Director, Save the Persecuted Christians*

Wayne Laugesen, Editorial Board Editor, *The Gazette* published in Denver and Colorado Springs

John Leake, Co-author, *The Courage to Face COVID-19: Preventing Hospitalization and Death While Battling the Bio-Pharmaceutical Complex*

David Legates, PhD, Former Delaware State Climatologist; former professor of Climatology, University of Delaware; co-author, *Hot Talk, Cold Science: Global Warming's Unfinished Debate*

Dr. John Lenczowski, PhD, Former Director of Soviet and European Affairs, National Security Council; founder, former President and Chancellor, Institute of World Politics; and author of Full-Spectrum Diplomacy and Grand Strategy*

Xiaoxu Sean Lin, PhD, Survivor of the Tiananmen Square massacre; former U.S. Army officer and Laboratory Director of Viral Diseases Branch, Walter Reed Army Institute of Research; and Assistant Professor, Feitian College*

Dr. Kat Lindley, MD, Board-certified family physician with a direct primary care practice in Texas; President, Texas Osteopathic Medical Association; member, American Academy of Physicians and Surgeons; participant in the Global Covid Summit

Reggie Littlejohn, Esq., Founder and President of Women's Rights Without Frontiers; Co-Chair of the Stop Vax Passports Task Force*

Lara Logan, award-winning investigative journalist; former CBS News' Chief Foreign Affairs Correspondent; and a host of "60 Minutes"

Trevor Loudon, Author and filmmaker, *The Enemies Within* and *The Enemies Within the Church*; contributor and podcaster, *Epoch Times**

John Paul Mac Isaac, Owner of the computer repair shop engaged by Hunter Biden

Dr. Robert Malone, M.D., M.S., Inventor of the mRNA technology and author of *Lies My Government Told Me and the Better Future Coming*

Colonel Robert Maness, U.S. Air Force (Ret.), former Commanding Officer of a bomber squadron; former Vice Commander of America's largest Airborne Intelligence Wing; former Commander, Kirtland Air Force Base; host, *The Rob Maness Show**

Dr. Tom Marks, PhD, Lansdale Chair of Irregular Warfighting Strategy, National Defense University; author, *People's War: Variants and Responses*

Jenny Beth Martin, Co-founder and National Coordinator, Tea Party Patriots; columnist, *Washington Times*; co-author, *Tea Party Patriots: The Second American Revolution*

David Matas, Esq., Canadian international human rights lawyer; co-founder, International Coalition to End Transplant Abuse in China; co-author, 2006 report and subsequent book entitled, *Blood Harvest: The Killing of Falun Gong for their Organs*; nominated for a Nobel Peace Prize in 2010

Caleb Max, Co-founder of the Athenai Institute, freedom-fighter focused on removing Chinese Communist Party influence from college campuses and educating the next generation of leaders on the dangers posed by the CCP

Aimee Villella McBride, Advocacy Liaison, Children's Health Defense

Marci McCarthy, Chairman, DeKalb County, Georgia GOP; past member, DeKalb County Board of Elections Voter Review Panel; President of Tech Exec Network

Faith McDonnell, Director of Advocacy, Katartismos Global; Co-Leader: Anglican Persecuted Church Network and the Global Anglican Fellowship Suffering Church Network; columnist/blogger, Patheos Evangelical Channel; and co-author *Girl Soldier: A Story of Hope for Northern Uganda's Children**

Warner Mendenhall, Esq., Founder, Mendenhall Law Group; founder of Health Freedom Counsel

Colonel John Mills, U.S. Army (Ret.): Former Special Forces operator; civilian Senior Executive Director for Cybersecurity Policy, Office of the Secretary of Defense; Senior Fellow, Center for Security Policy; author, *The Nation Will Follow: Firsthand Experiences Fighting the Deep State and the Action Plan for the American Citizen**

Julie Millsap, Government Relations Officer, Uyghur Human Rights Project

Steven Mosher, Founder and President, Population Research Institute; Author, *The Politically Incorrect Guide to Pandemics* and *Bully of Asia: Why China's Dream is the New Threat to World Order**

Colonel Grant Newsham, U.S. Marine Corps (Ret.), Former Marine

Attaché in Japan; former Foreign Service Officer; former East Asia-based corporate executive; Senior Fellow, Center for Security Policy*

Dr. Christiane Northrup, MD, Women's Health Expert, Health Pioneer, Wellness Speaker, and New York Times Best-Selling Author

J.R. Nyquist, Strategist; essayist; and author, *Origins of the Fourth World War* and co-author, *The New Tactics of Global War: Reflections on the Changing Balance of Power in the Final Days of Peace*; JRNyquist.blog*

Dr. Ian Oxnevad, PhD, Research Associate, National Association of Scholars and co-author of *After Confucius Institutes: China's Enduring Influence on American Higher Education*

Cleo Paskal, Non-Resident Senior Fellow for the Indo-Pacific, Foundation for Defense of Democracies; member, the International Board of Advisors of the Global Counter-Terrorism Council; instructor at Defense Colleges in the United Kingdom, India and Oman

Honorable Matthew Pottinger, Former Deputy National Security Advisor to the President; former National Security Council Asia Director; former Marine Corps intelligence officer; former *Wall Street Journal* reporter and Distinguished Visiting Fellow, Hoover Institution

Dr. Scott Powell, PhD , Senior Fellow, Discovery Institute; author, *Covert Cadre* and *Rediscovering America: How the National Holidays Tell an Amazing Story About Who We Are**

Dr. Sally Priester, MD, Specialist in Disaster Medicine

Dr. Peter Vincent Pry, PhD, Former Analyst, Central Intelligence Agency; former Professional Staff Member, House Armed Services Committee; former Chief of Staff, Congressional EMP Commission; former member, Strategic Forces Commission; author, *Blackout Warfare: Attacking the U.S. Electric Grid—A Revolution in Military Affairs* and *The Power and the Light: The Congressional EMP Commissions War to Save America 2001-2020***

Pam Pryor, Former senior official in State Department's Bureau Official for International Organizational Affairs; former Senior Advisor to the Under Secretary for Civilian Security, Democracy, and Human Rights; and Senior Fellow, Center for Security Policy

Dr. Michael Rectenwald, PhD , Former Marxist Professor, New York

University; author, *Thought Criminal* and *Beyond Woke*

Chanel Rion, White House Correspondent, One America News Network

Chad Robichaux, Marine Force Reconnaissance combat veteran; Founder and President, Mighty Oaks Foundation; author, *Unfair Advantage and Saving Aziz: How the Mission to Save One Became a Calling to Save 17,000*

Roger Robinson, Co-Founder and President, Prague Security Studies Institute; former Senior Director for International Economic Affairs, National Security Council; former Chairman and Vice Chairman, U.S.-China Economic and Security Review Commission; former Vice President and Special Assistant to the Chairman, Chase International Manhattan Bank

James Roguski, Author, activist and essayist, Substack.com and StoptheWho.com

Maria Luisa Rossi Hawkins, Italian journalist; Correspondent for *Mediaset*

Robby Stephany Smith Saunders, Former Special Assistant, State Department's International Organizations Bureau; former Legislative Director and National Security Advisor for Rep. Chip Roy; National Security Advisor, Coalition for a Prosperous America

Dr. Mark Schneider, PhD, Former career Senior Executive in the Department of Defense; former Foreign Service Officer; former Professional Staff Member, Senate Select Committee on Intelligence; Senior Analyst, National Institute for Public Policy*

Dr. William Schneider, PhD, Former Under Secretary of State for Science, Security Assistance and Technology; former Associate Director for National Security and International Affairs, Office of Management and Budget; former Chairman, Defense Science Board; President, International Planning Services; Senior Fellow, Hudson Institute*

Peter Schweizer, Investigative Journalist; President, the Government Accountability Institute; author, *Red-Handed: How American Elites Get Rich Helping China Win*

Colonel/Dr. Lawrence Sellin, PhD , U.S. Army (Ret.), former medical researcher and international businessman

Zubayra Shamseden, China Outreach Coordinator, Uyghur Human

Rights Project

Lee Smith, Investigative journalist for *The Tablet, The Federalist* and *Real Clear Investigations*; author of *The Permanent Coup: How Enemies Foreign and Domestic Targeted the American President* and *The Plot Against the President: The True Story of How Congressman Devin Nunes Uncovered the Biggest Political Scandal in U.S. History*

Sam Sorbo, Host of "The Sam Sorbo Show"; author, *They're Your Kids: An Inspirational Journey from Self-Doubter to Home-school Advocate* and *Words for Warriors: Fight Back Against the Crazy Socialists and the Toxic Liberal* Left; actress; filmmaker

Stephen Soukup, Author, *The Dictatorship of Woke Capital: How Political Correctness Captured Big Business* and publisher of the *Political Forum*

Brigadier General/Dr. Robert Spalding, U.S. Air Force (Ret.), PhD, former Chief China Strategist for the Chairman of the Joint Chiefs of Staff; former Senior Director for Strategic Planning at the National Security Council; and author, *Stealth War: How China Took Over While America's Elite Slept* and *War Without Rules: China's Playbook for Global Domination**

Gani Stambek, Kazakh human rights activist and freedom-fighter

Representative Chris Stewart, U.S. Air Force (Ret.), Member, House Permanent Select Committee on Intelligence and Appropriations Committees; entrepreneur; author, *The Final Fight for Freedom: How to Save Our Country from Chaos and War*

Dr. Bradley Thayer, PhD, Director for China Policy, Center for Security Policy; co-author, *Understanding the China Threat* and *How China Sees the World: Han Centrism and the Balance of Power in International Politics**

Dr. James Thorp, MD, Specialty in Obstetrics and Gynecology, Maternal and Fetal Medicine

David Tice, Partner, Moran Tice Capital Management; filmmaker, "Grid Down, Power Up"

Enghebatu Togochog, Director of Southern Mongolian Human Rights and Information Center, member, Captive Nations Coalition of the Committee on the Present Danger: China

Dr. Torsten Trey, MD, Founder, Doctors Against Forced Organ Harvesting (DAFOH.org); author, *An Unprecedented Evil Persecution: A Genocide Against Goodness in Humankind*

Honorable Francisco Tudela, Former First Vice President, Foreign Minister and UN Ambassador of Peru

Matthew Tyrmand, Investigative and editorial journalist; political strategist; activist; consultant; and investment banker

Jay Valentine, Professional data fraud-buster; CEO Contingency Sales. Com; columnist, *Software Executive Magazine Online*

Ann Vandersteel, co-chair of the Zelenko Freedom Foundation

Xi Van Fleet, Survivor of Mao's Cultural Revolution; opponent of Critical Race Theory indoctrination in Loudoun County schools and elsewhere

Dr. Elizabeth Lee Vliet, MD, President and CEO, Truth for Health Foundation; Preventive and Climacteric Medicine; author of *It's My Ovaries, Stupid!* and *Screaming to Be Heard: Hormone Connections Women Suspect and Doctors Still Ignore*

Zach Vorhies, Google Whistleblower; Software Engineer; author, *Google Leaks: An Expose of Big Tech Censorship*

Lieutenant Colonel Tommy Waller, U.S. Marines Reserves (Ret.), Combat Marine Force Reconnaissance veteran; and President and CEO of the Center for Security Policy and the Executive Director of its Secure the Grid Coalition

Dave Walsh, Managing Director, Takotagroup, LLC; former President & CEO, Mitsubishi Hitachi Power Systems; former Senior Executive, Westinghouse Electric

Bill Walton, Former CEO, Allied Capital; Chairman, Resolute Protector Foundation; Host, *The Bill Walton Show*, Senior Fellow, Discovery Institute's Center on Wealth, Poverty and Morality*

Benjamin Weingarten, Senior Contributor, *The Federalist*; Fellow, the Claremont Institute; author, *American Ingrate: Ilhan Omar and the Progressive-Islamist Takeover of the Democratic Party*

Dr. Naomi Wolf, PhD, author of *The Bodies of Others: The New Authoritarians, COVID-19 and the War Against the Humans*; founder and CEO of Daily Clout; Rhodes Scholar and Yale Graduate

Lieutenant Colonel Dakota Wood, U.S. Marine Corps (Ret.), combat Marine Veteran; Senior Research Fellow, Defense Programs, Heritage Foundation; Editor and co-author: *The 2023 Index of U.S. Military Strength*

Dr. Michael Yeadon, PhD, former Vice-President and Chief Scientific Officer for Allergic and Respiratory Diseases worldwide for the drug company, Pfizer. He is the co-founder and former CEO of the biotech company Ziarco.

Michael Yon, Army Green Beret veteran; combat correspondent; author, *Danger Close* and *Moment of Truth in Iraq*; photographer

Liz Yore, Esq., Former General Counsel and Director of the International Division of the National Center for Missing and Exploited Children; former General Counsel, Illinois Department of Children and Family Services; President and founder, Yore Children

Garrett Ziegler, Publisher, Marcopolousa.org; former staff member, White House Office of Trade and Manufacturing

---

*   Member, Committee on the Present Danger: China
** Deceased Member, Committee on the Present Danger: China

The Indictment-relevant Webinars – 2022

 Vanishing Sovereignty: The CCP's Takeover of Mongolia and the Rest of the World, Se Hoon Kim with Frank Gaffney, **Enkhbaat Toochog and Baasan Geleg, Esq., CPDC, (22** December 2022), *https://presentdangerchina.org/webinar-vanishing-sovereignty-ccps-takeover-of-mongolia-and-the-rest-of-the-world/*

 Civil-Military Fusion: The CCP's Whole-of-Society Warfare Against Us – and Americans' Enabling of It, Frank Gaffney with Gordon G. Chang, Charles "Sam" Faddis, Colonel Lawrence Sellin, Stephen Soukup, and John Guandolo, CPDC, (20 December 2022), *https://presentdangerchina.org/webinar-civil-military-fusion-the-ccps-whole-of-society-warfare-against-us/*

 *China's Covid Protests: Is Freedom Near?* Se Hoon Kim with Chris Chapell and Gordon Chang, CPDC, (16 December, 2022), *https://presentdangerchina.org/webinar-chinas-covid-protests-is-freedom-near/*

 Is Joe Biden a CCP 'Controlled Asset'? The Evidence from Hunter's Laptop; Deep-dive by Garrett Ziegler Makes the Case Our National Security is Imperiled, Frank Gaffney with Brian Kennedy and Garrett Ziegler, CPDC, (15 December 2022), *https://presentdangerchina.org/webinar-is-joe-biden-a-ccp-controlled-asset-the-evidence-from-hunters-laptop/*

The CCP 'Goes Nuclear': The Truth About Its Breakout Buildup; Experts Fact-find Pentagon Report Low-balling the Growing Chinese Threat, Frank Gaffney with Dr. Mark Schneider, Richard Fisher, LtG Stephen Kwast (Ret.), Hon. Robert Joseph, Dr. Philip Karber, Dr. Matthew Kroenig, CPDC, (7 December 2022), *https://presentdangerchina. org/webinar-the-ccp-goes-nuclear-the-truth-about-its-breakout-buildup/*

Qui Bono? CCP Bono – Climate Change Reparations – A Case Study; Experts Assess Team Biden's Marxist Wealth Redistribution Gambit, Frank Gaffney with Dr. David Legates, Dave Walsh, Myron Ebell, Hon. Robert Charles, Esq., CPDC, (1 December 2022), *https://presentdangerchina.org/webinar-qui-bono-ccp-bono-climate-change-reparations-a-case-study/*

TikTok Timebomb: The CCP's Virtual Weapon Platform Growing Chorus Recognizes Addictive App as National Security Treat, Urges Ban, Frank Gaffney with BG Robert Spalding, Connie Elliott, Colonel John Mills (USA Ret.), Joe Allen. With video clips: Sens. Tom Cotton and Mark Warner, and FBI Dir. Christopher Wray, and FCC Commissioner Brandon Carr, CPDC, (22 November 2022), *https:// presentdangerchina.org/webinar-tiktok-timebomb/*

Efficiency or Enslavement? Smart Health Cards, Digital Drivers Licenses, and Central Bank Digital Currency, Frank Gaffney and Reggie Littlejohn with Dr. Robert Malone, Leo Hohmann, Zach Vorhies, Dede Laugesen, and Connie Elliott, CPDC-SVPTF, (21 November 2022), *https:// presentdangerchina.org/webinar-efficiency-or-enslavement/*

Xi and Biden: Who's on America's Side; What's Next? – The Ominous Bali Summit and its Likely Repercussions, Frank Gaffney with Dr. Bradley Thayer, Hon. Pete Hoekstra, Captain James Fanell (Ret.), Dr. Michael Rectenwald, CPDC, (15 November 2022), *https://presentdangerchina.org/webinar-xi-and-biden-whos-on-americas-side-whats-next/*

The CCP is at War with America – What Are We Going to Do to Win? – Next Steps for Congressional Select Committee on China, Frank Gaffney with Dr. Bradley Thayer, Peter Schweitzer, Gordon G. Chang, and Brian Kennedy, CPDC, (8 November 2022), *https://presentdangerchina.org/the-ccp-is-at-war-with-america-what-are-we-going-to-do-to-win/*

Emperor Xi's Colonial Buildout – The Belt and Road Gambit for Enslaving the World, Frank Gaffney with Steve Mosher, Joseph Humire, Dr. Stephen Blank, Se Hoon Kim, Christine Douglass-Williams, and Nathan Carson, CPDC, (3 November 2022), *https://presentdangerchina.org/webinar-emperor-xis-colonial-build-out-the-belt-and-road-gambit-for-enslaving-the-world/*

The Biden Wrecking Operation: Harming America, Benefiting the CCP—A Damage Assessment Domestically and Internationally, Frank Gaffney with Colonel John Mills (USA Ret.), Kevin Freeman, Dave Walsh, LTC Dakota Walsh, Dr. Robert Malone, Ben Bergquam, and Dr. Bradley Thayer, CPDC, (1 November 2022), *https://presentdangerchina.org/webinar-usa-betrayed-the-biden-wrecking-operation-weakening-america-benefiting-the-ccp/*

The CCP's 'Whole-of-Society' Spying on America — Our Defense Requires No Less an Effort, Frank Gaffney with Nicholas Eftimiades, Hon. Pete Hoekstra, Charles "Sam" Faddis, and Colonel Grant Newsham, CPDC, (27 October, 2022), *https://presentdangerchina.org/webinar-unrestricted-warfare-the-ccps-whole-of-society-spying-on-america/*

This Land is Your Land, This Land is Their Land: Who's Selling Strategic American Real Estate to the CCP?; Unacceptable Enabling of Chinese Threats to our Homeland and National Security, Frank Gaffney with Hon. Kenneth Cuccinelli, Nathan Carson, Dr. Scott Powell, Kyle Bass, and Ross Kennedy, CPDC, (25 October 2022), *https://presentdangerchina.org/webinar-usa-betrayed-this-land-is-your-land-this-land-is-their-land-whos-selling-strategic-american-real-estate-to-the-ccp/*

U.S. Elections 'with Chinese Characteristics': Foreign and Domestic Exploitation of America's Electoral Vulnerabilities, Frank Gaffney with Jenny Beth Martin, Marci McCarthy, Colonel John Mills, Jay Valentine, and Charles "Sam" Faddis, CPDC, (20 October 2022), *https://presentdangerchina. org/webinar-unrestricted-warfare-u-s-elections-with-chinese-characteristics/*

Taking Down Our Liberties: January 6th and the Real Enemy Within, Frank Gaffney with Dr. Darren Beattie, Hon. Louie Gohmert, Trennis Evans, Edward Haugland, and Lara Logan, CPDC, (18 October 2022), *https://presentdangerchina.org/taking-down-our-liberties-january-6th-and-the-real-enemy-within/*

Crashing the CCP Party Congress, Frank Gaffney and Reggie Littlejohn with Debbie Georgatos, Gordon Chang, Dr. Simone Gold, Charles "Sam" Faddis, Lara Logan, Dede Laugesen, and Evan Sayet, CPDC Event, (15 October 2022), *https://presentdangerchina.org/crashing-the-ccp-party-congress-live-from-dallas/*

Fentanyl Genocide—The CCP's Chemical Warfare against America, Frank Gaffney with Dr. Bradley Thayer, Todd Bensman, Wayne Laugesen, and Sheriff Bill Elder, CPDC, (12 October 2022), *https://presentdangerchina.org/webinar-fentanyl-genocide-the-ccps-chemical-warfare-against-america/*

Enemies Within the Church: Taking Down America by Taking Down Faith, Frank Gaffney with Kevin Freeman, Rev. Kevin Jessip, Trevor Loudon, Dede Laugesen, Stephen K. Bannon, and Faith McDonnell, CPDC, (11 October 2022), *https://presentdangerchina.org/webinar-usa-betrayed-enemies-within-the-church/*

The CCP's Ominous 'Overseas Police Service Centers', Frank Gaffney with Lieutenant General William "Jerry" Boykin, Charles "Sam" Faddis, Hon. Kenneth DeGraffenreid, Colonel Dan Gallington, John Guandolo, and Hon. Robert Charles, Esq., CPDC, (6 October 2022), *https://presentdangerchina.org/webinar-unrestricted-warfare-the-ccps-ominous-overseas-police-service-centers/*

Taking Down the Border, Taking Down America, Frank Gaffney with Todd Bensman, Michael Yon, Trayce Bradford, and Ben Bergquam, CPDC, 4 October 2022), *https://presentdangerchina.org/webinar-usa-betrayed-taking-down-the-border-taking-down-america/*

The Last Hurdle for CCP Hemispheric Hegemony: Taking Down Free Brazil, Frank Gaffney, Matthew Tyrmand, Allan Dos Santos, Charles Gerow, and Francisco Tudela, CPDC, (29 September 2022), *https://presentdangerchina.org/webinar-unrestricted-warfare-the-last-hurdle-for-ccp-hemispheric-hegemony-taking-down-free-brazil/*

Covid Coercion and Fraud, Frank Gaffney and Reggie Littlejohn with Dr. Naomi Wolf, Warner Mendenhall, esq., Stephanie de Garay, Dr. Henry Ealy, John Beaudoin, Sr., and Sasha Latypova, CPDC-SVPTF, (28 September 2022), *https://presentdangerchina.org/webinar-covid-coercion-and-fraud/*

The CCP's Laptop from Hell, Frank Gaffney with John Paul Mac Isaac, Chanel Rion, LTG Jerry Boykin, and Rep. Chris Smith, CPDC, (27 September 2022), *https://presentdangerchina.org/usa-betrayed-the-ccps-laptop-from-hell/*

The CCP's Not-so-secret Weapon: 'Elite Capture', Frank Gaffney with Steven Mosher, Peter Schweizer, Charles "Sam" Faddis, and Trevor Loudon, CPDC, (22 September 2022), *https://presentdangerchina.org/webinar-unrestricted-warfare-the-ccps-not-so-secret-weapon-elite-capture/*

Decoupling From China: Stop Underwriting Our Enemy, Se Hoon Kim with Enes Kanter Freedom, Rep. Louie Gohmert, and Roger Robinson, CPDC-CNC Event, (20 September 2022), *https://presentdangerchina.org/livestream-decoupling-from-china-stop-underwriting-our-enemy/*

The CCP's March Through the International Institutions, Frank Gaffney with Dr. Bradley Thayer, Hon. Pete Hoekstra, Dr. Steven Hatfill, James Roguski, and Trevor Loudon, CPDC, (15 September 2022), *https://presentdangerchina.org/webinar-unrestricted-warfare-the-ccps-march-through-the-international-institutions/*

Pulling the Plug: Who's Helping the CCP to Take Down U.S. Energy Security?, Frank Gaffney with Dr. Bradley Thayer, Dave Walsh, Lieutenant Colonel Tommy Waller, and Brian Kennedy, CPDC, (13 September 2022), *https://presentdangerchina.org/webinar-usa-betrayed-pulling-the-plug-whos-helping-the-ccp-take-down-u-s-energy-security/*

On America's Families by the CCP and Its Friends, Frank Gaffney with Xi Van Fleet, Reggie Littlejohn, Esq., Dr. Robert Malone, M.D., Elizabeth Yore, Esq., Lieutenant General William "Jerry" Boykin, and Sam Sorbo, CPDC, (8 September 2022), *https://presentdangerchina.org/webinar-unrestricted-warfare-on-americas-families-by-the-ccp-and-its-friends/*

Formula for Fratricide: Biden's 'Othering' of MAGA, Frank Gaffney with Dede Laugesen, Dr. Michael Rectenwald, Charles "Sam" Faddis, Trevor Loudon, and Brian Kennedy, CPDC, (7 September 2022) *https://presentdangerchina.org/webinar-usa-betrayed-formula-for-fratricide-bidens-othering-of-maga/*

The CCP's Plans for an Ethnic Fifth Column?, Frank Gaffney with Gordon G. Chang, Esq., Dr. Sasha Gong, Dr. Xiaoxu Sean Lin, and Xi Van Fleet, CPDC, (1 September 2022), *https://presentdangerchina.org/webinar-unrestricted-warfare-the-ccps-plans-for-an-ethnic-fifth-column/*

The CCP's Pen Pals: The U.S. Media as Enablers of America's Mortal Enemy, Frank Gaffney with Prof. Kerry Gershaneck, Lance Crayon, Benjamin Weingarten, and Lee Smith, CPDC, (30 August 2022), *https://presentdangerchina.org/webinar-usa-betrayed-the-ccps-pen-pals-the-u-s-media-as-enablers-of-americas-mortal-enemy/*

The CCP's Belligerent 'Wolf Warrior Diplomacy', Frank Gaffney with Hon. Matthew Pottinger, Hon. Robert Joseph, Hon. Douglas Feith, Esq., Hon. Robert Charles, Esq., and Colonel Grant Newsham, CPDC, (25 August 2022), *https://presentdangerchina.org/webinar-unrestricted-warfare-the-ccps-belligerent-wolf-warrior-diplomacy/*

Covid Injections and Women: Miscarriage, Infertility, and More, Frank Gaffney and Reggie Littlejohn with Dr. James Thorp, MD, Dr. Elizabeth Lee Vliet, MD, Dr. Naomi Wolf, PhD., Dr. Jessica Rose, PhD, MSc, BSc, Dr. Evelyn Griffin, MD, and Dr. Christiane Northrup, M.D., CPDC-SVPTF, (24 August 2022), *https://presentdangerchina.org/webinar-covid-injections-and-women-miscarriage-infertility-and-more/*

Team Biden's Enabling of the CCP, Frank Gaffney with Brian Kennedy, Trevor Loudon, Kevin Freeman, Lieutenant General William "Jerry" Boykin, Dede Laugesen, Dr. Xiaoxu Sean Lin, PhD, and Dr. Bradley Thayer, PhD, CPDC, (23 August 2022), *https://presentdangerchina.org/webinar-usa-betrayed-captured-elites-team-bidens-enabling-of-the-ccp/*

The CCP's 'People's War' Against America, Frank Gaffney with Dr. Tom Marks, PhD, Dr. Michael Rectenwald, PhD, Xi Van Fleet, Trevor Loudon, and Connie Elliott, CPDC, (18 August 2022), *https://presentdangerchina.org/webinar-unrestricted-warfare-the-ccps-peoples-war-against-america/*

The China Model: Imposing in America the CCP's Toxic Pandemic Response, Frank Gaffney with Dr. Steven Hatfill, Dr. Robert Malone, John Leake, and Reggie Littlejohn, CPDC, (16 August 2022), *https://presentdangerchina.org/webinar-usa-betrayed-the-china-model-imposing-in-america-the-ccps-toxic-pandemic-response/*

Our Supply Chain Vulnerabilities, Frank Gaffney with Kevin Freeman, Nathan Carson, Rosemary Gibson, Shali Kumar, and Colonel John Mills, CPDC, (11 August 2022), *https://presentdangerchina.org/webinar-unrestricted-warfare-our-supply-chain-vulnerabilities/*

Biden's Takedown of America's Military, Frank Gaffney with Lieutenant General Robert "Rod" Bishop, Captain James Fanell, Colonel Robert Maness, U.S. Air Force, (Ret.), Richard Fisher, and Elaine Donnelly, CPDC, (9 August 2022), *https://presentdangerchina.org/webinar-usa-betrayed-bidens-takedown-of-americas-military/*

The CCP is Inside our (Electrical) Wire, Frank Gaffney with Lieutenant Colonel Tommy Waller, Texas State Sen. Bob Hall, and Kevin Freeman, CPDC, (4 August 2022), *https://presentdangerchina.org/webinar-unrestricted-warfare-the-ccp-is-inside-our-electrical-wire/*

The Abiding CCP Trojan Horses on America's Campuses, Frank Gaffney with Dr. Ian Oxnevad, PhD, Dr. John Lenczowski, PhD, Trevor Loudon, and Caleb Max, CPDC, (2 August 2022), *https://presentdangerchina.org/webinar-usa-betrayed-the-abiding-ccp-trojan-horses-on-americas-campuses/*

The CCP's "No Limits Partnership" with Putin's Russia, Frank Gaffney with J.R. Nyquist, Captain James Fanell, (USN Ret.), Charles "Sam" Faddis, Col. John Mills, (USA Ret.), and Dr. Bradley Thayer, PhD, CPDC, (28 July 2022), *https://presentdangerchina.org/webinar-the-ccps-unrestricted-warfare-and-its-no-limits-partnership-with-putins-russia/*

Covid Jabs: They're Coming for Your Babies, Frank Gaffney with Dr. Pierre Kory, Dr. Paul Alexander, Ph.D., Ernest Ramirez, Steve Kirsch, Dr. Sally Priester, and Aimee Villella McBride, CPDC-SVPTF, (26 July 2022), *https://presentdangerchina.org/webinar-covid-jabs-theyre-coming-for-your-babies/*

Who is Helping the CCP Take Down America's Food Security?, Frank Gaffney with Lieutenant Colonel Tommy Waller, USMC Reserves, Ross Kennedy, and Nathan Carson, CPDC, (26 July 2022), *https://presentdangerchina.org/webinar-usa-betrayed-who-is-helping-the-ccp-take-down-americas-food-security/*

The CCP's "Unrestricted Warfare" in Outer Space, Frank Gaffney with Lieutenant General Steven Kwast, U.S. Air Force (Ret.), Brigadier General Robert Spalding, U.S. Air Force (Ret.), Dr. Greg Autry, PhD, and Richard Fisher, CPDC, (21 July 2022), *https://presentdangerchina.org/the-ccps-unrestricted-warfare-in-outer-space/*

Who is Underwriting the CCP's "Unrestricted Warfare"?, Frank Gaffney with Roger W. Robinson, Will Hild, Stephen Soukup, Bill Walton, Kelley Currie, Robby Stephany (Smith) Saunders, CPDC, (19 July 2022), *https://presentdangerchina. org/webinar-usa-betrayed-who-is-underwriting-the-ccps-unrestricted-warfare/*

The CCP's Unrestricted Warfare in Latin America, Frank Gaffney with Joseph Humire, Hon. Francisco Tudela, and Victor González, CPDC, (14 July 2022), *https:// presentdangerchina.org/webinar-the-ccps-unrestricted-warfare-in-latin-america/*

Selling U.S. Strategic Oil Reserves to the CCP is Selling Out America, Frank Gaffney with Charles "Sam" Faddis, Dave Walsh, Captain James Fanell, USN (Ret.), and Kevin D. Freeman, CPDC, (12 July 2022), *https://presentdangerchina. org/webinar-selling-u-s-strategic-oil-reserves-to-the-ccp-is-selling-out-america/*

The CCP's Unrestricted Warfare in the Western Pacific, Frank Gaffney with Cleo Paskal, Colonel Grant Newsham (USMC Ret.), and Captain Bill Hamblett (USN Ret.), CPDC, (7 July 2022), *https://presentdangerchina.org/webinar-the-ccps-unrestricted-warfare-in-the-western-pacific/*

The CCP is at War with America, Frank Gaffney with Hon. Pete Hoekstra, Dr. Steven Hatfill, Kevin D. Freeman, LTG William "Jerry" Boykin, Colonel John Mills, J.R. Nyquist, and Brian T. Kennedy, CPDC, (30 June 2022), *https://presentdangerchina.org/webinar-the-ccp-is-at-war-with-america/*

How NOT to Deter War with the CCP, Frank Gaffney with Steve Mosher, Captain James Fanell (USN Ret.), and Dr. Bradley Thayer, PhD, CPDC, (16 June 2022), *https://presentdangerchina.org/webinar-how-not-to-deter-war-with-the-ccp/*

The Digital Gulag at Davos and the WHO: The Fight Continues, Frank Gaffney and Reggie Littlejohn with Leo Hohmann, Steve Kirsch, David Bell, James Roguski, Jay Valentine, Hon. Pete Hoekstra, CPDC-SVPTF, (13 June 2022), *https://presentdangerchina.org/webinar-the-digital-gulag-at-davos-and-the-who-the-fight-continues/*

The Enemies Within — Biden, Larry Fink, and Other CCP-captured Elites, Frank Gaffney with Trevor Loudon, Will Hild, Xi Van Fleet, Peter Schweitzer, Charles "Sam" Faddis, CPDC, (9 June 2022), *https://presentdangerchina.org/webinar-the-enemies-within-biden-larry-fink-and-other-ccp-captured-elites/*

The CCP's Death Camps Exposed, Frank Gaffney with Se Hoon Kim, Julie Millsap, and Kalbinur Gheni, CPDC, (2 June 2022), *https://presentdangerchina.org/webinar-the-ccps-death-camps-exposed/*

The CCP is Transitioning to War: What are We Doing?, Frank Gaffney with Brian Kennedy, Jeff Nyquist, and Dr. Bradley Thayer, CPDC, (25 May 2022), *https://presentdangerchina.org/webinar-the-ccp-is-transitioning-to-war-what-are-we-doing/*

Preventing a CCP Invasion of Taiwan, Frank Gaffney with Dr. Stephen Bryen, Secretary Seth Cropsey, and Colonel Grant Newsham, CPDC, (19 May 2022), *https://presentdangerchina.org/webinar-preventing-a-ccp-invasion-of-taiwan/*

Stop the Sellout of US Sovereignty to the WHO, Frank Gaffney and Reggie Littlejohn with Pam Pryor, Dr. Peter Breggin, James Roguski, Leo Hohmann, Trevor Loudon, Nick Corbishley, Michelle Bachman, Hon. Pete Hoekstra, Faith McDonnell, CPDC-SVPTF, (16 May 2022), *https://stopvaxpassports.org/webinar-stop-the-sellout-of-us-sovereignty-to-the-who/*

No TSP for CCP: No U.S. Pension Funds for the Chinese Communist Party, Frank Gaffney with Roger Robinson, Kyle Bass, Joel Caplan, and LTG William "Jerry" Boykin, CPDC, (12 May 2022), *https://presentdangerchina.org/webinar-no-tsp-for-ccp-no-thrift-savings-plan-for-the-chinese-communist-party/*

DIGITAL GULAG: Vaccine Passports, "Disinformation", **and a Cashless Society,** Frank Gaffney and Reggie Littlejohn with Nick Corbishley, Zach Vorhies, Joe Allen, Kevin Freeman, and Connie Elliott, CPDC-SVPTF, (2 May 2022), *https:// stopvaxpassports.org/webinar-digital-gulag-vaccine-passports-and-a-cashless-society/*

Silence and Oppression: Discussion on Uyghurs in Saudi **Arabia,** Se Hoon Kim with Zubayra Shamseden, Julie Millsap, and Abduweli Ayup, CPDC-CNC, (23 April 2022), *https://presentdangerchina.org/webinar-silence-and-oppression-discussion-on-uyghurs-in-saudi-arabia/*

Preventing Nuclear War: This is No Drill, Frank Gaffney with Brian Kennedy, Jeff Nyquist, Dr. Mark Schneider, Dr. William Schneider, Dr. Robert Joseph, Dr. Peter Vincent Pry, Lieutenant Colonel Chuck Devore, (USA Ret.), Peter Huessy, Reggie Littlejohn, Esq., and Colonel John Mills (USA Ret.), CPDC, (23 March 2022), *https://presentdangerchina.org/ webinar-preventing-nuclear-war/*

COVID MANDATES: Destroying the Military & Deep **Sixing the Evidence**, Frank Gaffney and Reggie Littlejohn with Thomas Renz, Esq., Dr. Scott Sturman, Justin Butterfield, Esq., Chad Robicheaux, Hayden Robicheaux, Colonel Robert Maness (USAF Ret.), and Lieutenant General William "Jerry" Boykin (USA Ret.), CPDC-SVPTF, (15 February 2022), *https://stopvaxpassports.org/webinar-covid-mandates-destroying-the-military-deep-sixing-the-evidence/*

Covid Mandates: Crushing the Faithful, Frank Gaffney and Reggie Littlejohn with Kevin Jessie, Dr. Kevan Kruse, Trevor Loudon, Mike Berry, esq., Rachel Keane, Dr. Sr. Dierdre Byrne, CPDC-SVPTF, (20 January 2022), *https://stopvaxpassports. org/webinar-covid-mandates-crushing-the-faithful/*

The Indictment-relevant Webinars – 2023

 Oh, Canada: The CCP's Subversion of Our Northern Neighbor – and Us, Frank Gaffney with Jan Jekielek, Michel Juneau-Katsuya, Charles "Sam" Faddis, Scott McGregor, CPDC, (21 March 2023), *https://presentdangerchina.org/webinar-oh-canada-the-ccps-subversion-of-our-northern-neighbor-and-us/*

 No Drill: The CCP is Preparing for a Shooting War, Frank Gaffney with Gordon G. Chang, Ross Kennedy, Charles "Sam" Faddis, Kevin Freeman, Dr. Bradley Thayer, CPDC, (16 March 2023), *https://presentdangerchina.org/no-drill-the-ccp-is-preparing-for-a-shooting-war/*

 Who's on First at the WHO: The CCP Runs It – and We Must Leave It, Frank Gaffney with Jonathan Emord, Esq. JD, Dr. Robert Malone, M.D., Dr. David Bell, Reggie Littlejohn, Esq. JD, James Roguski, Honorable Michele Bachmann, CPDC, (7 March 2023), *https://presentdangerchina.org/webinar-whos-on-first-at-the-who-the-ccp-runs-it-and-we-must-leave-it/*

 Xi's 'Zero-RoI' Strategy: If There's a Shooting War, Will Americans Lose All Investments in China?, Frank Gaffney with Kevin Freeman, CFA, Joel Caplan, Colonel Grant Newsham (USMC Ret.), Bill Walton, Brian T. Kennedy, CPDC, (28 February 2023), *https://presentdangerchina.org/webinar-xis-zero-roi-strategy/*

 Every Breath You Take: Big Brother's Plan to Stalk You through the WHO, Frank Gaffney with Reggie Littlejohn, Esq. JD, Dr. Michael Yeadon, PhD, Dr. Francis Boyle, PhD, Trevor Loudon, Dr. David Bell, Ann Vandersteel, CPDC-SVPTF, (27 February 2023), *https://presentdangerchina.org/webinar-every-breath-you-take-big-brothers-plan-to-stalk-you-through-the-who/*

Is Ukraine the CCP's First Front? Is the PRC Arming Russia and the Prospects for a Second Front in the Pacific, Frank Gaffney with Dr. Phillip Karber, PhD, Dr. Stephen Blank, PhD, Hon/Lt Col Chuck DeVore, (USA Ret.), Col. John Mills (USA Ret.), Dr. Bradley Thayer, PhD, CPDC, (23 February 2023), *https://presentdangerchina.org/webinar-is-ukraine-the-ccps-first-front/*

Does the CCP Think It Can Fight and Win a Nuclear War?; Experts Evaluate the Evidence — and the Implications — if the Answer is 'Yes', Frank Gaffney with Richard Fisher, Mark Schneider, PhD, and Phillip Karber, PhD, CPDC, (16 February 2023), *https://presentdangerchina.org/webinar-does-the-ccp-think-it-can-fight-and-win-a-nuclear-war/*

Lessons from Beijing's Balloon Belligerence: The CCP's Full-on Espionage, Its Wider Unrestricted Warfare and How to Respond, Frank Gaffney with Richard Fisher, Ambassador Henry Cooper, PhD, Lieutenant General William "Jerry" Boykin (USAF Ret.), Colonel Robert Maness (USAF Ret.), Trevor Loudon, Colonel John Mills (USA Ret.) CPDC, (7 February 2023), *https://presentdangerchina.org/webinar-lessons-from-beijings-balloon-belligerence/*

War-Footing: A Top U.S. General Orders War Preparations to Deter the CCP; Will the Rest of the Military Do the Same? Frank Gaffney with Lieutenant General William "Jerry" Boykin, Captain James Fanell (USN Ret.), Colonel Robert Maness (USAF Ret.), Colonel Grant Newsham (USMC Ret.), Colonel Derek Harvey (USA Ret.), Dr. Bradley Thayer, PhD, CPDC, (2 February 2023), *https://presentdangerchina.org/webinar-war-footing-a-top-u-s-general-orders-war-preparations-to-deter-the-ccp/*

President of World Mongol Federation, Hon. Tsakhiagiin Elbegdorj, CPDC-CNC Event, (26 January 2023), *https://presentdangerchina.org/former-president-of-mongolian-peoples-republic-hon-tsakhiagiin-elbegdorj-speaks-at-our-event/*

Countering CCP Hegemony: Mongolia's Fight to be Free, Frank Gaffney with Hon. Tsakhiagiin Elbegdorj, Dr. Bradley Thayer, PhD., Se Hoon Kim, Enghebatu Togochog, CPDC-CNC Event, (26 January 2023), *https://presentdangerchina. org/webinar-countering-ccp-hegemony-mongolias-fight-to-be-free/*

Digital Gulag: The WHO's Proposed Amendments to the International Health Regulations, Reggie Littlejohn, esq. with Trevor Loudon, Dr. Peter Breggin, MD, James Roguski, Pam Pryor, CPDC-SVPTF, (18 January 2023), *https:// presentdangerchina.org/webinar-digital-gulag-the-whos-proposed-amendments-to-the-international-health-regulations/*

The CCP Runs the Table Throughout the Western Hemisphere: Implications for the USA and the Region, Frank Gaffney with Dr. Bradley Thayer, PhD, Matthew Tyrmand, Christine Douglass-Williams, Charles Gerow, Gordon Chang, Colonel Grant Newsham (USMC Ret.), CPDC, (16 January 2023), *https://presentdangerchina.org/webinar-the-ccp-runs-the-table-throughout-the-western-hemisphere/*

Will China lose if it Invades Taiwan? Frank Gaffney, Colonel Mark Cancian, Captain James Fanell (USN Ret.) Colonel Grant Newsham (USMC Ret.), Colonel John Mills (USA Ret.), Dr. Bradley Thayer, PhD, CPDC, (12 January 2023), *https://presentdangerchina.org/webinar-will-the-ccp-lose-if-it-attacks-taiwan/*

Organ Genocide: The CCP's Industrial-scale Murder of Its Unwanted, Frank Gaffney with Dr. Torsten Trey, David Matas, Esq., Dr. G. Weldon Gilcrease, MD, CPDC, (5 January, 2023), *https://presentdangerchina.org/webinar-the-ccps-organ-genocide/*

No Drill: The CCP Is Preparing for a Shooting War – To Prevent It, We Better Do the Same

In addition to the Committee on the Present Danger: China's webinars concerning the Chinese Communist Party's pre-kinetic "unrestricted warfare" against America and those here who have enabled it, we have also addressed the question of whether Xi Jinping is willing to engage in violent aggression against our friends and allies, and perhaps us.

The most recent such webinar was conducted on March 16, 2023. It was entitled "No Drill: The CCP is Preparing for a Shooting War; To Prevent It, We Better Do the Same." The program featured comments from the following extraordinary authorities: China expert Gordon G. Chang; food security and supply chain specialist Ross Kennedy; former CIA operative Charles "Sam" Faddis; economic warfare maven Kevin Freeman; and historian and strategist Dr. Bradley Thayer PhD.

The following are highlights of their contributions:

Frank Gaffney (Moderator): We are joined today for a very important purpose, perhaps the most important of all: to assess the evidence that is now available that the Chinese Communist Party is prepared to move beyond the "unrestricted warfare" that it has engaged in for decades.... There is evidence, if we have the wit and the will to look for it, that the Chinese are preparing for a new phase of this war, a shooting war. And that evidence is sometimes hiding in plain sight. It is sometimes something that you have to have a bit of expertise to ferret out.

And in most cases, you need people with backgrounds relevant to making sense of what the intelligence community calls "indicators and warnings" to understand just how grave the present moment is in terms of the prospect that the Chinese Communist Party is indeed, not only a mortal enemy of this country, but one determined to translate its long time aspiration to destroy the United States of America into action, potentially with truly catastrophic effects.

We say all this not to terrify people into passivity or a fetal pose, but rather in the hopes that we can empower those watching this program, and especially your elected representatives and those appointed by your elected representatives, to act *now*. We believe there may still be time to deter the shooting war the Xi Jinping regime has in mind for us and if necessary, to defeat their attacks, should they come.

We have assembled, as usual, an extraordinary group of participants to bring those kinds of skills to bear, to illuminate the evidence that's out there and to help interpret it and to give us specific ideas about what we must be doing now to try to have this come out as well as possible for us and for freedom- loving people around the world, more generally.

* * *

Gordon Chang: Frank has asked me to talk about the mobilization of China's civilians for war. To do this, though, I'd like to have a little bit of context in terms of where the Chinese regime is going. And I want to start in October at the Communist Party's 20th National Congress there. Xi Jinping gave a very dark speech to open that momentous event. And during that time, he received extensions. He got his third term to be general secretary of the Communist Party and as important, his third term as chairman of the party's central military commission, which controls the military.

At the time, it looked like he had total power. But we saw after that a number of events that suggested that his opponents inside the regime were actually making ground against him. But at the just concluded National People's Congress. Xi Jinping got his third term as president of the Chinese state. Now, this is a ceremonial post, but it's significant because it appears that by getting this and some other things that have occurred in the last 3 or 4 days that Xi Jinping has actually consolidated power and that he has been able to rein in his opponents.

This is significant because now Xi Jinping is not hearing *any* moderate voices that are restraining his thirst for military adventurism. And this thirst for military adventurism is fueled in large part by an extreme ideological antagonism he has for the United States.

So, that means that the words that we have heard recently have meaning. Now at the National People's Congress meeting and at the twin meeting of China's top advisory body, Xi Jinping gave a very dark assessment of the world. Plus, he also and this was unusual, he pointed out the United States and is establishing justifications for striking us because we had been constraining him confronting China, all the rest of it.

And then we also heard just today Xi Jinping speech closing the session, which also talked about the Chinese military as being the protector of China, which we've heard before, but also in much more assertive language. This is in the context of a speech that the new foreign minister, Chin Gong, gave on March 7th, [in which he] actually talked about how, if the United States did not back down, there would "surely be conflict and confrontation." And Chin Gong also talked about "catastrophic consequences."

That is in the context in which we have to view what the Chinese regime has in fact, been doing recently. You know, we all know that Xi has been sponsoring the fastest and the largest military buildup since the Second World War. At the Communist Party's 20th National Congress in October, he appointed what is now called his "war cabinet."

Xi Jinping has [also] been trying to sanction-proof his regime. And this is the subject of today's talk.

We have seen Xi Jinping try to mobilize China's civilians for war. We go back to the first day of 2021, that's the day that amendments to China's national defense law went into effect. Those amendments took power away from the state council, which is a civilian body, and they gave them to the Communist Party Central Military Commission. And these amendments were facilitating the mobilization of China's civilians for war.

Then, on the first day of this month, China's new reservist law went into effect. And pursuant to that, the Party is now establishing across the country what are called National Defense Mobilization Offices.

Really what we're seeing is China making putting together the infrastructure for mobilization of civilian society. In July of last year, a Chinese entrepreneur told me that he was making medical products for the civilian sector. This entrepreneur told me that Communist Party cadres had visited him and demanded that he convert his production lines in China to away from civilian products in order to make products for the Chinese military. Communist Party cadres had been visiting other factories and also demanding that those private owners as well convert to military production. And in fact, this entrepreneur said that the party was now operating factories that once were privately owned – so many of them, because of these demands, that the factory owners just had decided that they were not going to stick around for what they called Xi Jinping's war.

So, we're hearing the war talk. We are seeing changes in the Chinese political system and we're seeing what Chinese officials are in fact, doing. And that puts into context all of these disturbing developments because you will hear a lot of China experts who are extremely knowledgeable say, "Well, you know, all this war talk is just sort of bluffing, it's "Empty Fortress," which is an allusion to a series of events in Chinese history where people just sort of bluff their way with war talk.

But I actually think that now this war talk has meaning. We see China making great preparations to go into battle. And at the same time we see in the US a lack of a sense of urgency and a lack of perception of what is happening inside China.

And this is not just President Biden. This is also the three and four stars in the Pentagon and people across the American political system. And I'm talking about not only liberal Democrats, but also conservative Republicans. So, we have failure across the American political system to understand what is happening inside China and why we must prepare as well.

So, I fear that there will be war between China and the United States. And I believe that there *will* be war, unless something changes. And right now, I don't see anything changing. So we do smell war in the air and we know that nothing good can come of this.

Ross Kennedy: There is a Chinese proverb that says "May you live in interesting times." And I don't know that it's a proverb. Maybe it's intended as a curse, but we certainly do find ourselves in interesting times. And one of the really key understandings that we must have here is that China has become an enemy unlike any other, or an adversary, if you will, to the United States. It's the first really pacing adversary we have [had] that has the ability to overmatch us…, not just militarily.

* * *

But for me, for my view, [and] for a lot of people who have come to understand…the pandemic and post-pandemic world, it's the logistics and the supply chain piece that really tell the tale of where the vulnerabilities are in the dynamic that has emerged between the US and China and the peer competition. And there's really three things that if you focus on those almost exclusively, you'll get to an 80% answer – not only on knowing what the risks are or what the opportunities are, but also what the future state looks like because it's physical things that we can track.

It's physical things that we can count. It's physical things that we know are moving or not moving that give us probably the greatest and most accurate granular assessment of where any entity, whether it's a company, whether it's an individual, or whether it's a country is at.

And that's food, water and energy. Those are the three most basic things. If there was a, you know, a Maslow's hierarchy of needs, of geopolitical stability or geopolitical predictability, those three would be where we would begin.

My particular specialty is in the food and water side. …China's moves in India, Nepal, Tibet, all of that makes sense when you look at [it] in the context of wanting to really monopolize the source of water for much of Asia, which is the Himalayan mountain range.

But talking about food here in particular, fossil fuel-derived fertilizers, things like ammonium nitrate, things like urea, they have undergone serious restrictions to the point that we would probably categorize that as hoarding behavior [by the CCP] and [it has] been doing so for about two-and-a-half to three years. Restriction of export into the global market, but also restrictions on sales and allocations internally within China across the provinces of who gets what, when and where. They're doing the same thing with exports of fresh and frozen protein grains as well.

The one that's probably most concerning is that the United States, the West in general – with the exception of DSM and BASF in Europe – have allowed China to conquer and really corner the global market on synthetic vitamins. And these aren't just the kind of vitamins that we mix a bunch together in Little Flintstone tablets. These are massive large-scale production of vitamin powders and granules that go into commercial animal production or commercial animal feed. It's mixed into the ration. Animals must have this. I do not encourage anybody to go looking for vitamin A or vitamin E deficiency in animals and what those pictures might look like. But it is it is an ugly picture in some cases.

And in other ways, it dramatically blunts the competitive advantage that the United States has developed in terms of calories per capita that we have. China out-produces us on pork and chicken and others on raw kilograms, but their population is so high that the US actually produces more calories from an agriculture side than any other country in the world. Without vitamins, though, that advantage on the animal protein side degrades to a place where we would be looking at anywhere from a 7-to-9-times increase on meat, dairy and egg prices....

About 90% of all the vitamins in the world are made there. It's a dirty process. It's one that gets sideways when it's not done correctly. It gets sideways of all manner of environmental laws that we have in the US. And so we don't do it here. We've allowed it to be outsourced.

It's also very natural gas intensive, which is why BASF very recently announced plans to relocate large parts of their vitamin production from the corporate headquarters in Germany that's serviced by Gazprom natural gas *to China*. They didn't come to the US with our abundant amount of natural gas or potential natural gas abundance. They went to China.

So...[Germany is] one of the linchpins of our military security alliance in Europe, one that we have been counting on to pull [its] weight, which they have not done economically or militarily for quite some time. But we largely have pretended [that's so] as a matter of policy. Yet, they have chosen to invest a multi-billion dollar expansion of their vitamin production in China, not in the US. And BASF is telling us that's their bet on the future.

Amino acids is the same. Amino acids are lysine, threonine, valine, isoleucine methionine, the building-blocks of life. Large parts of the global supply are also made in China. About 60% of global production. Most of these are derived from a fermentation process that's fed by corn milling. So, the corn mills produce a sugar product like dextrose. It can be refined into high fructose corn syrup or in its raw form can be fed to bacteria that are genetically engineered to feed on sugar. And they excrete amino acids, whatever they're programmed to do biologically. Those amino acids are dried. They're packaged, powdered and shipped around the world. And they are another essential component, just like vitamins and animal feed.

China of late has been very openly within the industry discussing what it *will* look like – not what it *could* look like, not if – *when* they begin the process of embargoing exports of amino acids and vitamins to the US.

Two of the last indicators that show that China is moving more towards a war-footing in terms of ensuring domestic availability of supply at the expense of the world and trade partners:

[First,] we're starting to see unusual patterns of shipping activity related to ocean carriers, steamship lines, bulk vessels, bulk tankers. China is hoarding as much of the long-term charter capacity as possible. They're starting to build ocean vessels that are ostensibly for global maritime trade for large carriers like a Maersk or COSCO, China's own massive state-owned enterprise that builds ships but also operates ship lines.

But they're starting to build these under terms that allow China and Chinese lenders who pay for these multi-hundred-million- dollar vessels [providing] that, at any time the operator or the charter party defaults on the agreement, they can be forced to move whatever, whenever or wherever as determined by the lender. They essentially seize control of the charter and force the company [that] is operating the ship that took the loan on the ship to carry what they want, where they want from the Chinese government side.

[Second,] we're also seeing finally an expansion of clearinghouse alternatives to SWIFT in the food and feed trades. This would be from the China side. This would be CIPS or Cross-border Interbank Payment System. It's a method of settling transactions. SWIFT allows [denomination] in certain approved currencies. It's a main sanction tool for the US against Russia.

As we've seen, it's probably not worked out quite the way we'd hoped in degrading their ability to fund military operations in Ukraine and throughout, you know, throughout Europe and Asia. CIPS has emerged as a way that non-US allies or adversaries or neutral parties even are able to clear transactions outside of the US dollar.

The US dollar is not going anywhere as the global reserve currency. It's still a phenomenally important tool of US economic and trade and national security policy. But China is now providing an alternative and they are slowly building their way towards that.

When we take these things into account, what we see is a clear pattern not only of manipulating markets for pricing purposes, as China has historically done.

What we're also seeing is an ability of China to starve or make the cost of protein and food and energy so high for the West that, if we don't disengage right now – starting with this farm bill and a Defense Production Act-like version of reshoring [things] of critical value-added, like agricultural food and feed production, to the United States – we are very quickly going to be looking at, maybe not a *famine*, but the most expensive on a per calorie basis we have probably ever seen food be in the United States. And that is not a storm we can weather politically or economically.

Charles "Sam" Faddis: When we start talking about the possibility of some sort of offensive military action by communist China, one of the things that troubles me is that I think we assume without really being conscious of it, that we're going to have some sort of perfect clarity into what is unfolding, what Beijing's intentions are, what actions they're taking.

At the heart of this, I guess, is the belief that this gigantic intelligence community that we have is collecting so much information that really we will have a full understanding of what's unfolding, and therefore, we're going to be able to react and move and make decisions based on all of this incredibly detailed information. And I think that it's really dangerous to rely upon that assumption for at least a couple of reasons:

The first is it assumes that the state of our collection on the Chinese target is robust, and I'm not sure at all where the evidence is for that. I would trot out as Exhibit A to the contrary, everything concerning COVID 19 and the Wuhan lab. Biological warfare programs, any kind of dangerous biological programs that could become biological warfare programs all across the world, are absolutely top-tier collection targets for the intelligence community. There's nothing more important than that.

The Communist Chinese are obviously our number one enemies on the face of the earth. The Wuhan lab is actually a couple of labs, but one of them is [China's] only BSL-4 lab. In other words, a top-tier lab in China, the kind of place where you can...work with the most dangerous organisms. So, you add all of that up and really, if you think about it, you should not have been able to sneeze inside the Wuhan lab back at the beginning of this pandemic without American intelligence knowing about it.

Between human sources, hacking, computer systems, and technical collection, we should have had this place wired in every conceivable way. And yet apparently, as far as we can tell, we got no warning whatsoever that there was an impending pandemic or even that a pandemic had begun really, until it was well under way.

So, we were apparently completely blind concerning a target that should have been absolutely at the very top of our list of priorities. That's not particularly encouraging. And then we should note that three years on, the best we can get out of the intelligence community are these sort of lukewarm assessments that, "Yeah, with moderate confidence maybe, probably, sort of, this thing started in that lab," right? None of that should fill you with confidence that we really have penetrated the Communist China in the way that we need to have.

Then [second], we add on top of this the capacity for the Chinese to feed us disinformation and misinformation and engage in deception operations. There's nothing new about those. They're really old. They're as old as the intelligence business, which has been around forever.

And we got lots and lots of examples of people all over the planet very effectively deceiving their opponents. We did this to the Germans in 1943 when we invaded Sicily, but we fed them all kinds of information in whole variety of ways, saying we were going to invade Greece. We did it again on an even grander scale in 1944. D-Day Operation Overlord General Patton put in charge of a completely fictitious army – replete with inflatable tanks and all of this stuff – to convince the Germans that we were coming across the Channel at a completely different location than, in fact, we did. So, this kind of stuff is done all the time. It's done very effectively. The Chinese are really, really good at it.

And if you combine those two things, their capacity to feed us a line in effect, and then our weak collection, that should not leave you feeling like, yeah, this war is going to start with us understanding exactly what's happening and when it's going to start and so forth.

In fact, I think very much to the contrary, what you ought to assume is that when and if we go to war with the Communist Chinese, it's going to look a lot like December 7th, 1941 or September 11th, 2001. It's going to be a complete surprise. And we are going to go from a standing start, having already been hit.

Kevin Freeman: If we could echo on what Sam Faddis concluded with, can you imagine if it were 1936 or 1939 rather than 2023? Now, 1936 was the year my mother was born. It was the middle of the Depression. It was a dust bowl hitting my home state of Oklahoma.

Now, if my mother had lived, she would be just eighty-seven years old. So, it's really not that long ago. And lots of people alive today were alive eighty-seven years ago. That was a strange time. And it's strange to look back on.

It's hard to believe. But corporate America was heavily investing in Germany, considered a European powerhouse, the Nazi Party was seen as fostering an economic miracle. The Summer Olympics were held in Berlin. Leading Americans applauded the discipline and focus of Adolf Hitler. I know it sounds strange now, but it was true then.

In fact, there were many prominent Americans who supported the Nazis, and the Nazis had great influence in Washington, D.C., on college campuses and in the boardrooms of American corporations. Nazi Germany received huge investments from Americans in 1936, second only to Great Britain, well ahead of France and any other nation. Now, that seems really bizarre and strange. I share that, though, because it was a foolish thing to fund the Nazi war machine and millions of people paid for it with their lives.

It's also foolish to invest in any enemy with whom we know we will soon be at war. Can you imagine how those investors fared or how the companies that had grown dependent on Germany were crushed when war broke out? We were at war with Germany within five years of 1936. But, according to Air Force General Mike Minihan, we don't have that long with China, maybe *two* years. Can we learn from history what happens if we go to war with China next year or the year after?

It was in 2013 that Xi Jinping rose to power. Shortly afterward, he made it official Chinese policy to de-Americanize the world, and that was written in an official CCP publication. They've been prepping for this for ten years. Five years ago, I published a blog series at GlobalEconomicWarfare.

com with the title "The Winds of War."

It detailed why and how we would soon be at war with China and also a proxy war with Russia. Here's a direct quote that I wrote in 2018: "China has been prepping for a war-footing. There are multiple clues that, when they are pieced together, suggest a combination attack plan using economic pressure, technology and physical invasion to assert Chinese dominance in Asia and ultimately over the planet. It is no longer acceptable to naively overlook this reality."

Now that [draws] on congressional testimony I gave in 2016 when I testified with Gordon Chang in Congress, and I wrote, as Confucius supposedly said, "There cannot be two suns in the sky."

The goal under President Xi is to displace the United States so that China can take her rightful place, controlling at least one- third of the world's economy and overseeing the rest. Now consider this from ZeroHedge on March 7th: They said, "In an unexpectedly sharp escalation of diplomatic rhetoric, China's foreign minister said that the US should change its distorted attitude towards China or conflict and confrontation will follow." [He] defend[ed] the country's stance on the war in Ukraine and its close ties with Russia.

Let me translate that for you: [Foreign Minister Chin Gong] was saying, "Let us do what we want or we will start a hot war." And in his same speech, he threatened the US dollar and he made clear their intentions for Taiwan.

So, let me ask this question: If it were 1939 and you knew what was about to happen in World War Two, would you want to buy German goods or invest your pension with the Nazis? It sounds ridiculous, but that's exactly what Americans are doing right now with Communist China. Some people estimate we've invested upwards of $3 trillion total when you count stock purchases, plus all the hidden ways that China extracts capital through the global index funds. Does this seem wise?

The worst part is that we've been funding their innovation. As an example, consider last month's report from the Center for Security and Emerging Technology. They said collectively observed transactions involving American investors totaled $40.2 billion, invested in 251 Chinese artificial intelligence companies, which accounts for 37% of the $110 billion raised by all Chinese AI companies. That's just for artificial intelligence. And 37% of the money invested came from deals involving American investors and 91% of that venture capital money.

That's not counted in the totals that I shared earlier, the $3 trillion bottom line, we're funding China to the tune of trillions of dollars in total. And much of that is helping China get ahead of us. It used to be China was relegated to imitation. But after stealing so much American tech and getting so much investment, they nearly caught up and may soon surpass us. And that's what we see with artificial intelligence.

The scary thing is that China is directly using these capabilities to expand their war machine. Consider the front-page headline from the *Daily Mail* this month. They said, "China increases its military budget by 7.1%, $230 billion to boost combat preparedness for major tasks, amid fears it will launch an invasion of Taiwan."

Remember, by law, every Chinese company must serve the CCP, and that means the People's Liberation Army, as well. Thus, the defense budget can literally be any percentage of the economy that the CCP wants, regardless of the official numbers, and we're seeing the impact.

Now we hear from Dr. Mark Mobius, perhaps the world's most famous emerging market investor, that he's unable to get his money out of China. I worked with Mark when we were both at Templeton, and I even joined him on a research trip to China in 1999. Here's what he said [recently]:

I have an account with HSBC in Shanghai. I can't take my money out. The government is restricting the flow of money out of the country. I can't get an explanation for why they're doing this. They're putting up all kinds of barriers. They don't say, No, you can't get your money out. But they say, give us all the records from the 20 years of how you made this money. This is crazy.

Mobius also said that the CCP has taken golden shares in every company to gain absolute control. That's just what the Nazis did.

Now I'm going to share with you six things that we should do at the national and international level. And if we work together, we can make a difference, because all of this points to a hot war.

First, we must immediately put a brake on funding China. Full stop. Our friend Roger Robinson believes that this would rattle the shaky Chinese economy and win the war by itself. Roger directed Reagan's economic warfare team so he knows who he's talking about. That means we've got to block the thrift savings plan from China, just like the Trump team did. But it also means we can't invest anything through index funds or even at the personal level into Chinese companies.

At the personal level, you should watch Economic War Room atEconomicWarRoom.com and find a financial advisor who can help you get out of China. Now, on February 9th, according to the New York Times, the Biden administration said they had plans to curb investments into China. Well, that was great. But two weeks later, there were reports that the Biden administration is scaling back on any plans to reduce investment in China. Why? That's a huge mistake. We must sharply curtail and even pull back investments wherever possible.

Step number two, though, explains maybe the "Why?" We have to root out, expose and eliminate Chinese infiltration. We must listen to Peter Schweitzer. If politicians are compromised, they have to go. This includes President Biden. Congress better look at the Hunter Biden laptop because it certainly appears his family has been compromised by Chinese money.

We have to shut down all the Confucius Institutes or any efforts by China to influence our college campuses. And we have to eliminate Chinese funded research in American institutions.

Number three, we need to demand reparation from China for the way they handled the COVID pandemic. China won't pay, of course, but at least taking this step gives us the moral courage to push back elsewhere. And it could bring in allies.

Number four, in conjunction with steps two and three, we must root out Chinese influence in international organizations like the World Health Organization, or we should pull entirely out of the World Health Organization.

Five, because we know the Chinese plan to attack the dollar, we've got to strengthen it. This means we must develop a proper energy policy. We can no longer afford the pie in the sky, green energy policies that fund Chinese solar and wind companies.

Instead, we have to build American pipelines to develop our internal energy, exporting as needed for allies. In addition, we need to draft a sensible budget and stick to it. We need growth policies while restricting federal spending. The Republicans have a plan for this. But we need [to do] that. Otherwise the dollar will come under sharp attack. And we've seen what happened with Silicon Valley Bank. We need to correct this *now*.

Finally, we need to follow the advice of that great Latin phrase. Si vis pacem, para bellum. Roughly translated, If you seek peace, prepare for war. This means we must build up our own defenses. We must also review our supply chains for industry and replace Chinese components… It's not going to be easy.

Overall, it's going to be a huge undertaking and we haven't much time. But if China sees our resolve, we could actually avert war. But that means getting on a war-footing, now rather than later. Remember, peace through strength. It's time for that again. Now, you can learn more about this by watching Economic War Room. We cover this every week on our episodes.

Dr. Bradley Thayer: What I'd like to do is focus on two major components that haven't been as addressed as yet, and that's the political and the military elements. [We] began the discussion by reviewing intelligence failures and the risks that are associated and indicators that we may receive. Much of the conversation today is centered around strategic indicators of attack. And these are indicators that, if you will, are deeper causes or deeper indicators rather than tactical indicators, for example, that a missile is on its way to Taiwan or to the United States.

These are the CCP's efforts to lay the foundation, to lay the groundwork for the attack. What I would like to do is look at the political first. The political elements are what the CCP is doing with respect to allies and with respect to its messages.

So we can see that the CCP is employing its allies – now Russia – to occupy NATO and the United States in Ukraine and is working assiduously with Russia to establish markets, obviously for Russian energy, for Russian economic goods, but also to support Russia militarily in combat in the war with Ukraine. So, Russia serves a very important political purpose for the CCP.

Iran does as well. We have witnessed in the last few months Xi has been very active in the Middle East, going to Saudi Arabia, and to some degree, working with the UAE and with Iran. Importantly, and we see Xi is attempting...to eliminate the petrodollar, but also to ensure energy supply that China will have secure energy supplies from Russia, but also from the Gulf sheikhdoms, Saudi Arabia and most importantly, Iran. So, he's working with his allies to establish that foundation very importantly.

Xi's also working with allies in South America, elsewhere in Latin America, in Cuba and [with] cartels in Mexico to undermine the United States, [our] population, but also to undermine American security in the Western Hemisphere, as well as globally.

Moreover, [at] the National People's Congress that we have had this week and his speech [on] March 15th...Xi Jinping introduced his idea of the Global Civilizational Initiative – [an] effort to set the new strategic narrative for the future, to set new norms, principles, the rules of the road in international politics....He is seeking to advance, to take that away from the Anglo-American order that was established at the end of World War Two and that served us extremely well in the Cold War and after.

Xi is remaking the rules of international politics and of international organizations, and he's trying to bring CCP control over all of those elements. And Frank Gaffney and so many others have done great work in illuminating how the World Health Organization is operating as a pawn for the Chinese Communist Party. So we can see strategic indicators both in allies, but also in terms of how Xi's reaching [out] to global audiences to make the case for China's dominance, which will be very valuable in a competition with the United States, a war with the United States.

Xi is saying the future belongs to China. It no longer belongs to the United States and its allies, which again, is preparing the battlefield in a strategic sense for the conflict that's coming in a military sense.

What do we witness? We witness very alarming events. Most importantly, and I'll focus on Taiwan and on the US efforts on Taiwan. We have witnessed the routinization of Chinese military exercises opposite Taiwan, violations of Taiwan's airspace, as well as its seaspace through again a routinization of exercises, of violations to ensure that when the attack does come, and it is certain to come, that there is as little tactical warning as possible, surprise is maximized.

The cutting of the undersea cables in Matsu, for example, a small island off of Taiwan's coast, closer to China is another indication of how China is preparing the battlefield to cut off the ability of Taiwan to communicate with the rest of the world so that the CCP is able to maximize surprise.

With respect to the US, General Minihan's memo at the end of January of this year, when it was publicly leaked and then released later publicly, is telling. As Minihan argues, 2025 is the year of conflict, which he anticipates because at in October, at the 20th Party Congress, Xi in essence laid the groundwork for his subsequent term and he established his war council at that time.

Additionally, in 2024, Minihan argued, Taiwan has presidential elections and the US does, as well, compound[ing the difficulty of] our ability to respond as well as Taiwan's. So, Minihan made the case that 2025 would be the year of the invasion. I think that's a good indicator. It certainly may come sooner than 2025 as a result of Xi Jinping's motivation to conquer Taiwan as part of his larger plan of dethroning the United States of ejecting the United States from its position as the dominant state in international politics, the dominant state that has created world stability, a world economic order, and an international order that recognizes the freedoms of all people around the world.

The order that China is creating is the opposite of all of those elements. The behavior of the Chinese Communist Party is defined wherever it is present by exploitation of people and the environment. So, we're seeing in the political realm prodigious changes as Xi sets the battlefield and then in the military realm as well with minions.

…The spy balloon was a sign, a component of political warfare against the United States. [It] was not only collecting intelligence against important targets in the US, but signaling the American people and the American government that Xi will hit the homeland through ballistic missiles, cruise missiles, hypersonic missiles, COVID.

As we have witnessed, there are many avenues to hurt the American homeland, the American people. But the spy balloon was an indicator that the CCP is targeting the American people for destruction in their war, and it was a very important reminder of Xi's intent.

When we review the military and we review political components in conjunction to what my colleagues have already addressed, we see that in every area, in every realm, the CCP is preparing for war against US allies, US partners and against the United States, itself. And it compels all of those actors Taiwan, India, key allies like Japan, Australia, our NATO allies, as well as, of course, of the United States to prepare for conflict and to prepare for conflict *today*, military conflict against the CCP.

My colleagues have underscored that the CCP has been at war for us against the United States since it came to power in 1949, and we should certainly recognize that that war is going to take kinetic form and will do so very readily and far sooner than many individuals might anticipate as a result of Xi Jinping's determination to destroy the United States and the order that it created.

Our Team

The Committee on the Present Danger: China (CPDC) is an inde-' pendent, non-partisan effort to educate and inform American citizens and their policymaking representatives about the truly existential threats posed by the Chinese Communist Party. It is inspired by the original, 1970s-era Committee on the Present Danger, which helped make the case for the defeat of the Soviet Union – an initiative that one of its members, Ronald Reagan, sought an electoral mandate to achieve, and subsequently did.

The Committee's mission is to conceive, promote and secure the adoption of robust responses to the CCP's long-running unrestricted warfare against America. To an extent even greater than the Soviet Union in its heyday, Communist China imperils this country, its people and the last best hope for freedom worldwide. We seek to foster a new American consensus regarding the policies and priorities required to defeat this perilous challenge. For that purpose, the Committee has brought together an extraordinary array of experienced, skilled and patriotic experts on China, national security leaders, human rights activists and religious freedom champions. This book would not have been possible without their help and support and is intended to amplify its impact for a time such as this.

THE COMMITTEE'S CO-SPONSORS

The American Strategy Group

In December of 2015, Brian T. Kennedy, William J. Bennett and a group of national security scholars and writers founded the American Strategy Group. It is dedicated to understanding how the Chinese Communist Party, Vladimir Putin's Russia, Sharia-supremacism and the widespread deviation from America's founding principles are imperiling the United States and Western Civilization. Its purpose is to educate America's citizenry and policymakers about these threats, what must be done to defend the United States, and to recover the strategic seriousness that has long guided this nation. Its website is *www.amstrategy.org.*

The Center for Security Policy

The Center for Security Policy was founded in 1988 by Frank J. Gaffney and fellow veterans of the Reagan administration and Capitol Hill and other experienced national security practitioners. Over the past thirty-five years, it has promoted the proven practice of "peace through strength," spoken truth to power and creatively worked to protect our constitutional Republic from all enemies, foreign and domestic. Often it has done so by forging and fostering coalitions, "Team B's", working groups, task forces, etc. to perform successfully impactful tasks no single organization could realistically be expected to achieve. The Committee on the Present Danger: China is a preeminent example of such sponsored collaboration.

Brian Kennedy serves as the Chairman of the Committee on the Present Danger: China and Frank Gaffney as its Vice Chairman. Dede Laugesen, a highly experienced and accomplished freedom-fighter, is the Committee's invaluable Executive Secretary.

Endnotes

1 *The CCP's 'People's War' Against America,* Frank Gaffney with Dr. Tom Marks, PhD, Dr. Michael Rectenwald, PhD, Xi Van Fleet, Trevor Loudon, and Connie Elliott, CPDC, (18 August 2022), *https://presentdangerchina.org/webinar-unrestricted-warfare-the-ccps-peoples-war-against-america/*

2 *Determination of the Secretary of State on Atrocities in Xinjiang,* Press Statement, Michael R. Pompeo, Secretary of State, January 19, 2021, *https://2017-2021.state.gov/determination-of-the-secretary-of-state-on-atrocities-in-xinjiang/index.html*

3 *2020 Country Reports on Human Rights Practices: China,* March 30, 2021, https://www.state.gov/reports/2020-country-reports-on-human-rights-practices/china/

4 *Silence and Oppression: Discussion on Uyghurs in Saudi Arabia,* Se Hoon Kim with Zubayra Shamseden, Julie Millsap, and Abduweli Ayup, CPDC-CNC, (23 April 2022), *https://presentdangerchina.org/webinar-silence-and-oppression-discussion-on-uyghurs-in-saudi-arabia/*

5 *The CCP's Death Camps Exposed,* Frank Gaffney with Se Hoon Kim, Julie Millsap, and Kalbinur Gheni, CPDC, (2 June 2022), *https://presentdangerchina.org/webinar-the-ccps-death-camps-exposed/*

6 *Xinjiang: US seizes 'forced labour' Chinese hair imports, BBC News,* July 2, 2020, *https://www.bbc.com/news/world-asia-china-53259557*

7 *China Harvested Organs From Living People, Doctors Helped With Executions, Israeli Researcher Claims, Haaretz,* 10 April 2022, *https://www.haaretz.com/israel-news/2022-04-10/ty-article-magazine/.premium/research-china-harvested-organs-from-living-people-doctors-helped-with-executions/00000180-5bb8-df19-a7f3-db-fc53720000*

8 Statement by UN High Commissioner for Human Rights Michelle Bachelet after official visit to China, Office of the U.N. High Commissioner for Human Rights, 28 May 2022, *https://www.ohchr.org/en/statements/2022/05/statement-un-high-commissioner-human-rights-michelle-bachelet-after-official*

9 Planning Outline for the Construction of a Social Credit System (2014-2020), China Copyright and Media, Rogier Creemers, Posted on June 14, 2014 Updated on April 25, 2015, *https://chinacopyrightandmedia.wordpress.com/2014/06/14/planning-outline-for-the-construction-of-a-social-credit-system-2014-2020/*

10 See also, Lianchao Han and Dr. Bradley A. Thayer, PhD, *Understanding the China*

Threat, Routledge India, (30 September 2022), *https://www.amazon.com/Understanding-China-Threat-Lianchao-Han/dp/103211083X*

11 *Countering CCP Hegemony: Mongolia's Fight to be Free,* Frank Gaffney with Hon. Tsakhiagiin Elbegdorj, Dr. Bradley Thayer, PhD., Se Hoon Kim, Enghebatu Togochog, CPDC-CNC Event, (26 January 2023), *https://presentdangerchina.org/webinar-countering-ccp-hegemony-mongolias-fight-to-be-free/*

12 *Thanks China, now go home: buy-up of Zambia revives old colonial fears,* The Guardian, 5 Feb. 2007, *https://www.theguardian.com/world/2007/feb/05/china.chrismcgreal*

13 Ibid., *Silence and Oppression: Discussion on Uyghurs in Saudi Arabia*

14 *Deng Xiaoping's "24-Character Strategy",* Global Security, (28 Dec. 2013), *https://www.globalsecurity.org/military/world/china/24-character.htm*

15 Joint Address by MI5 and FBI Heads, Security Service MI5, (6 July 2022), *https://www.mi5.gov.uk/news/speech-by-mi5-and-fbi*

16 *The CCP's Last-ditch Gamble: Biological and Nuclear War, Epoch Times,* San Renxing, (5 Aug. 2005), *https://truthinchina.wordpress.com/2006/11/29/the-ccp%E2%80%99s-last-ditch-gamble-biological-and-nuclear-war/*

17 *China plans to invade US!,* transcript of a speech believed to have been given by Mr. Chi Haotian, Minster of Defense and vice-chairman of China's Central Military Commission, (15 February 2005), *https://www.military-quotes.com/forum/china-plans-invade-us-t16958.html*

18 *Unrestricted Warfare: China's Master Plan to Destroy America,* Qiao Liang, and Wang Xiangsui, Echo Point Books & Media, (Original: 1999; 10 November 2015), *https://www.amazon.com/Unrestricted-Warfare-Chinas-Destroy-America/dp/1626543054*

19 Ben Westcott, *Chinese media calls for 'people's war' as US trade war heats up,* CNN, (14 May 2019), *https://www.cnn.com/2019/05/14/asia/china-us-beijing-propaganda-intl/index.html*

20 *The CCP's 'People's War' Against America,* Frank Gaffney with Dr. Tom Marks, PhD, Dr. Michael Rectenwald, PhD, Xi Van Fleet, Trevor Loudon, and Connie Elliott, CPDC, (18 August 2022), *https://presentdangerchina.org/webinar-unrestricted-warfare-the-ccps-peoples-war-against-america/*

21 Ibid., *The CCP's 'People's War' Against America*

22 *Military-Civil Fusion and the People's Republic of China,* U.S. Department of State, (20 January 2021), *https://www.state.gov/wp-content/uploads/2020/05/What-is-MCF-One-Pager.pdf*

23 *Civil-Military Fusion: The CCP's Whole-of-Society Warfare Against Us—and Americans' Enabling of It,* Frank Gaffney with Gordon G. Chang, Charles "Sam" Faddis,

Col. Lawrence Sellin, Stephen Soukup, and John Guandolo, CPDC, (20 December 2022), *https://presentdangerchina.org/webinar-civil-military-fusion-the-ccps-whole-of-society-warfare-against-us/*

24 *[Top Secret Recording] War Mobilization Meeting of the Southern War Zone of the PLA: Guangdong Province in The State of War,* Jennifer Zeng, (17 May, 2022), *https://www.jenniferzengblog.com/home/2022/5/16/top-secret-recording-war-mobilization-meeting-of-the-southern-war-zone-of-the-pla-guangdong-province-is-in-a-state-of-war*

25 *The CCP is Transitioning to War: What are We Doing?,* Frank Gaffney with Brian Kennedy, Jeff Nyquist, and Dr. Bradley Thayer, CPDC, (25 May 2022), *https://presentdangerchina.org/webinar-the-ccp-is-transitioning-to-war-what-are-we-doing/*

26 Ibid., *Civil-Military Fusion: The CCP's Whole-of-Society Warfare Against Us—and Americans' Enabling of It*

27 *The CCP is at War with America,* Frank Gaffney with Hon. Pete Hoekstra, Dr. Steven Hatfill, Kevin D. Freeman, LTG William "Jerry" Boykin, Col. John Mills, J.R. Nyquist, and Brian T. Kennedy, CPDC, (30 June 2022), *https://presentdangerchina.org/webinar-the-ccp-is-at-war-with-america/*

28 *Sun Tzu*, Translated by Griffith, Samuel, B., Foreword by Hart, B.H. Liddell, *The Art of War*, Oxford: Oxford University Press, 1963, p. 77

29 Schweizer, Peter, *Red-Handed: How China Wins by Making American Elites Rich*, New York, Harper Collins, (2022), *https://www.amazon.com/Red-Handed-American-Elites-Helping-China/dp/0063061147*

30 *The CCP's Not-so-secret Weapon: 'Elite Capture',* Frank Gaffney with Steven Mosher, Peter Schweizer, Charles "Sam" Faddis, and Trevor Loudon, CPDC, (22 September 2022), *https://presentdangerchina.org/webinar-unrestricted-warfare-the-ccps-not-so-secret-weapon-elite-capture/*

31 Ibid., *The CCP's Not-so-secret Weapon: 'Elite Capture'*

32 Trevor Loudon, *THE ENEMIES WITHIN: Communists, Socialists and Progressives in the U.S. Congress*, CreateSpace, (24 July 2013), *https://www.amazon.com/ENEMIES-WITHIN-Communists-Socialists-Progressives/dp/1490575170*

33 Ibid., *The CCP's Not-so-secret Weapon: 'Elite Capture'*

34 Ibid., *The CCP's Not-so-secret Weapon: 'Elite Capture'*

35 See also, *The CCP's Laptop from Hell*, Frank Gaffney with John Paul Mac Isaac, Chanel Rion, LTG Jerry Boykin, and Rep. Chris Smith, CPDC, (27 September 2022), *https://presentdangerchina.org/usa-betrayed-the-ccps-laptop-from-hell/*

36 Ibid., *The CCP's Not-so-secret Weapon: 'Elite Capture'*

37 Background: Tony Blinken: Secretary of State, Accountability Initiative, (12 April 2021), *https://accountabilityinitiative.org/tony-blinken-secretary-of-state/*

38 Ibid., *The CCP's Not-so-secret Weapon: 'Elite Capture'*

39 See, *https://AccountabilityInitiative.org*

40 Ibid., *The CCP's Not-so-secret Weapon: 'Elite Capture'*

41 Ibid., *The CCP's Not-so-secret Weapon: 'Elite Capture'*

42 *The CCP's Pen Pals: The U.S. Media as Enablers of America's Mortal Enemy*, Frank Gaffney with Prof. Kerry Gershaneck, Lance Crayon, Benjamin Weingarten, and Lee Smith, CPDC, (30 August 2022), *https://presentdangerchina.org/webinar-usa-betrayed-the-ccps-pen-pals-the-u-s-media-as-enablers-of-americas-mortal-enemy/*

43 *The CCP is at War with America,* Frank Gaffney with Hon. Pete Hoekstra, Dr. Steven Hatfill, Kevin D. Freeman, LTG William "Jerry" Boykin, Col. John Mills, J.R. Nyquist, and Brian T. Kennedy, CPDC, (30 June 2022), *https://presentdangerchina. org/webinar-the-ccp-is-at-war-with-america/*

44 Declassified Assessment on COVID-19 Origins, The Office of the Director of National Intelligence (ODNI), (October 29, 2021), *https://www.dni.gov/files/ODNI/ documents/assessments/Declassified-Assessment-on-COVID-19-Origins.pdf*

45 *The CCP is at War with America: The Chinese Communist Party's COVID-19 Biological Warfare Attack and What's Next,* Peter Hoekstra, Lt. Gen. William "Jerry" Boykin (USA Ret.), Charles "Sam" Faddis, Kevin D. Freeman, Frank J. Gaffney, Dr. Steven Hatfill, MD, MSc, MSc, M.Med, Brian T. Kennedy, Col. John Mills (USA Ret.), J.R. "Jeff" Nyquist, Center for Security Policy and the Committee on the Present Danger: China (CPDC), (27 June, 2022), *https://www.amazon.com/ CCP-War-America-Communist-Biological-ebook/dp/B0B72HBDSR; https://ccpat-war.com*

46 Ibid., *The CCP is at War with America*

47 Ibid., *The CCP is at War with America*

48 *The China Model: Imposing in America the CCP's Toxic Pandemic Response,* Frank Gaffney with Dr. Steven Hatfill, Dr. Robert Malone, John Leake, and Reggie Littlejohn, CPDC, (16 August 2022), *https://presentdangerchina.org/webinar-usa-betrayed-the-china-model-imposing-in-america-the-ccps-toxic-pandemic-response/*

49 *The CCP's March Through the International Institutions,* Frank Gaffney with Dr. Bradley Thayer, Hon. Pete Hoekstra, Dr. Steven Hatfill, James Roguski, and Trevor Loudon, CPDC, (15 September 2022), *https://presentdangerchina.org/webinar-unrestricted-warfare-the-ccps-march-through-the-international-institutions/*

50 Ibid., *The CCP's March Through the International Institutions*

51 See: *Who's on First at the WHO: The CCP Runs It – and We Must Leave It,* Frank Gaffney with Jonathan Emord, Esq. JD, Dr. Robert Malone, M.D., Dr. David Bell, Reggie Littlejohn, Esq. JD, James Roguski, Hon. Michele Bachmann, CPDC, (7 March 2023), *https://presentdangerchina.org/webinar-whos-on-first-at-the-who-the-ccp-runs-it-and-we-must-leave-it* .

52 See: *Digital Gulag: The WHO's Proposed Amendments to the International Health Regulations*, Reggie Littlejohn, esq. with Trevor Loudon, Dr. Peter Breggin, MD, James Roguski, Pam Pryor, CPDC-SVPTF(18 January 2023), *https://presentdangerchina.org/webinar-digital-gulag-the-whos-proposed-amendments-to-the-international-health-regulations/* ; *Efficiency or Enslavement? Smart Health Cards, Digital Drivers Licenses, and Central Bank Digital Currency*, Frank Gaffney and Reggie Littlejohn with Dr. Robert Malone, Leo Hohmann, Zach Vorhies, Dede Laugesen, and Connie Elliott, CPDC-SVPTF, (21 November 2022), *https://presentdangerchina.org/webinar-efficiency-or-enslavement/* ; *The Digital Gulag at Davos and the WHO: The Fight Continues*, Frank Gaffney and Reggie Littlejohn with Leo Hohmann, Steve Kirsch, David Bell, James Roguski, Jay Valentine, Hon. Pete Hoekstra, CPDC-SVPTF, (13 June 2022), *https://presentdangerchina.org/webinar-the-digital-gulag-at-davos-and-the-who-the-fight-continues/* ; *DIGITAL GULAG: Vaccine Passports, "Disinformation", and a Cashless Society*, Frank Gaffney and Reggie Littlejohn with Nick Corbishley, Zach Vorhies, Joe Allen, Kevin Freeman, and Connie Elliott, CPDC-SVPTF, (2 May 2022), *https://stopvaxpassports.org/webinar-digital-gulag-vaccine-passports-and-a-cashless-society/*

53 Ibid., *The China Model: Imposing in America the CCP's Toxic Pandemic Response*

54 Ibid., *The China Model: Imposing in America the CCP's Toxic Pandemic Response*

55 *Efficiency or Enslavement? Smart Health Cards, Digital Drivers Licenses, and Central Bank Digital Currency*, Frank Gaffney and Reggie Littlejohn with Dr. Robert Malone, Leo Hohmann, Zach Vorhies, Dede Laugesen, and Connie Elliott, CPDC-SVPTF, (21 November 2022), *https://presentdangerchina.org/webinar-efficiency-or-enslavement/*

56 Ibid., *The CCP is at War with America*

57 Ibid., *The China Model: Imposing in America the CCP's Toxic Pandemic Response*

58 Frances Mao, *China abandons key parts of zero-Covid strategy after protests*, BBC News, (7 December 2022), *https://www.bbc.com/news/world-asia-china-63855508*

59 *Digital Gulag: The WHO's Proposed Amendments to the International Health Regulations*, Reggie Littlejohn, esq. with Trevor Loudon, Dr. Peter Breggin, MD, James Roguski, Pam Pryor, CPDC-SVPTF(18 January 2023), *https://presentdangerchina.org/webinar-digital-gulag-the-whos-proposed-amendments-to-the-international-health-regulations/*

60 Peter Schweizer, *Red-Handed: How American Elites Get Rich Helping China Win*, Harper, (25 January 2022), *https://www.amazon.com/Red-Handed-American-Elites-Helping-China/dp/0063061147*

61 *The Enemies Within — Biden, Larry Fink, and Other CCP-captured Elites*, Frank Gaffney with Trevor Loudon, Will Hild, Xi Van Fleet, Peter Schweizer, Charles "Sam" Faddis, CPDC, (9 June 2022), *https://presentdangerchina.org/webinar-the-enemies-within-biden-larry-fink-and-other-ccp-captured-elites/*

62 Ibid., *The Enemies Within — Biden, Larry Fink, and Other CCP-captured Elites*

63 Grady McGregor, '*The era is over for big rock stars': How Beijing's crackdown on Jack Ma forever changed the role of China's CEOs, Fortune,* (30 September 2022) , https:// fortune.com/2022/09/30/jack-ma-china-tech-crackdown-ceos/

64 *China's $1.3 Trillion Housing Crackdown Leaves Few Winners, Bloomberg Business-week,* (27 December 2022), https://www.bloomberg.com/news/articles/2022-12-28/-1-3-trillion-china-housing-crackdown-hasn-t-fixed-unaffordable-property-market

65 Logan Wright, *China's Slow-Motion Financial Crisis Is Unfolding as Expected,* Center for Strategic & International Studies, (21 September 2022), https://www.csis.org/ analysis/chinas-slow-motion-financial-crisis-unfolding-expected

66 Hudson Lockett, *How Xi Jinping is reshaping China's capital markets, Financial Times,* (11 June 2022), https://www.ft.com/content/d5b81ea0-5955-414c-b2eb-886dfed4dffe

67 *Xi's 'Zero-RoI' Strategy: If There's a Shooting War, Will Americans Lose All Investments in China?,* Frank Gaffney with Kevin Freeman, CFA, Joel Caplan, Colonel Grant Newsham (USMC Ret.), Bill Walton, Brian T. Kennedy, CPDC, (28 February 2023), https://presentdangerchina.org/webinar-xis-zero-roi-strategy/

68 Angel Au-Yeung, *U.S. Generals, Diplomats Want Chinese Companies Out of Their Retirement Plan,* (3 August, 2022) *Wall Street Journal,* https://www.wsj. com/articles/u-s-generals-diplomats-want-chinese-companies-out-of-their-retire-ment-plan-11659528001?reflink=desktopwebshare_permalink&st=hktj0lcfbSny9qi

69 Frank Gaffney, *President Trump Channels His Inner Reagan,* CPDC, (May 15, 2020), https://presentdangerchina.org/president-trump-channels-his-inner-reagan/

70 *Key legislators tell Federal Retirement Thrift Investment Board: Keep China out of U.S. government pensions,* CPDC Press Release, (Washington, D.C., 25 May 2022) https://presentdangerchina.org/release-key-legislators-tell-federal-retirement-thrift-in-vestment-board-keep-china-out-of-u-s-government-pensions/

71 Decoupling From China: Stop Underwriting Our Enemy, Se Hoon Kim with Enes Kanter Freedom, Rep. Louie Gohmert, and Roger Robinson, CPDC-CNC Event, (20 September 2022), https://presentdangerchina.org/livestream-decoupling-from-chi-na-stop-underwriting-our-enemy/

72 *No TSP for CCP: No U.S. Pension Funds for the Chinese Communist Party,* Frank Gaffney with Roger Robinson, Kyle Bass, Joel Caplan, and LTG William "Jerry" Boykin, CPDC, (12 May 2022), https://presentdangerchina.org/webinar-no-tsp-for-ccp-no-thrift-savings-plan-for-the-chinese-communist-party/

73 Roberto Suro, Not Chinese Agent, Chung Says: DNC fund-raiser Johnny Chung testifies Tuesday before a House committee investigating campaign finance, Wash-ington Post, (Wednesday, May 12, 1999; Page A2), https://www.washingtonpost. com/wp-srv/politics/special/campfin/stories/chung051299.htm

74 *China in the WTO: Past, Present, and Future,* World Trade Organization (December 2011), *https://www.wto.org/english/thewto_e/acc_e/s7lu_e.pdf*

75 Phelim Kine, *China joined rules-based trading system — then broke the rules,* Politico, (09 December 2021), *https://www.politico.com/news/2021/12/09/china-wto-20-years-524050*

76 *Our Supply Chain Vulnerabilities,* Frank Gaffney with Kevin Freeman, Nathan Carson, Rosemary Gibson, Shali Kumar, and Col. John Mills, CPDC, (11 August 2022), *https://presentdangerchina.org/webinar-unrestricted-warfare-our-supply-chain-vulnerabilities/*

77 Rosemary Gibson and Janardan Prasad Singh , *China Rx: Exposing the Risk of America's Dependence on China for Medicine,* Prometheus, (17 April 2018), *https://www.amazon.com/China-Rx-Exposing-Americas-Dependence/dp/1633883817*

78 Ibid., *Our Supply Chain Vulnerabilities*

79 *Who is Helping the CCP Take Down America's Food Security?,* Frank Gaffney with Lieutenant Colonel Tommy Waller, USMC Reserves, Ross Kennedy, and Nathan Carson, CPDC, (26 July 2022), *https://presentdangerchina.org/webinar-usa-betrayed-who-is-helping-the-ccp-take-down-americas-food-security/*

80 Michael J. de la Merced and David Barboza, Needing Pork, China Is to Buy a U.S. Supplier, New York Times, (29 May 2013), *https://archive.nytimes.com/dealbook.nytimes.com/2013/05/29/smithfield-to-be-sold-to-shuanghui-group-of-china/*

81 Michael Shields, *ChemChina clinches landmark $43 billion takeover of Syngenta,* Reuters, (4 May 2017), *https://www.reuters.com/article/us-syngenta-ag-m-a-chemchina/chemchina-clinches-landmark-43-billion-takeover-of-syngenta-idUSKBN1810CU*

82 Robert D. Atkinson, *State and local governments need to stop subsidizing Chinese companies,* The Hill, (21 April 2022), *https://thehill.com/opinion/finance/3275383-state-and-local-governments-need-to-stop-subsidizing-chinese-companies/*

83 Ibid., *Our Supply Chain Vulnerabilities*

84 Roberto Suro, Clinton Fund-Raiser to Plead Guilty: Yah Lin "Charlie" Trie walks to the federal courthouse in Little Rock, Ark., Washington Post, (May 22, 1999; Page A2), *https://www.washingtonpost.com/wp-srv/politics/special/campfin/stories/trie052299.htm*

85 Ibid., *Who is Helping the CCP Take Down America's Food Security?*

86 *CFIUS Says Chinese Investment in North Dakota Agricultural Land Is Outside Its Jurisdiction,* Holand & Knight, (24 January 2023), *https://www.hklaw.com/en/insights/publications/2023/01/cfius-determines-chinese-greenfield-investment-in-north*

87 Jaie Avila, *Texas stops Chinese billionaire from building wind farm,* News 4 San Antonio, (May 26th 2021), *https://news4sanantonio.com/news/trouble-shooters/legislature-passes-bill-to-prevent-chinese-billionaire-from-building-wind-farm*

88 Ibid., *This Land is Your Land, This Land is Their Land: Who's Selling Strategic American Real Estate to the CCP?*

89 Ibid., *This Land is Your Land, This Land is Their Land: Who's Selling Strategic American Real Estate to the CCP?*

90 Gov. Doug Burgum, *Burgum issues statement on Air Force letter citing 'significant threat' from Fufeng project in Grand Forks,* Office of the Governor of North Dakota, (31 January 2023), https://www.governor.nd.gov/news/burgum-issues-statement-air-force-letter-citing-significant-threat-fufeng-project-grand-forks

91 Joel Crane, *Fufeng corn milling plant project to be terminated; Air Force cites national security concerns,* Valley News Live, (Jan. 31, 2023), *https://www.valleynewslive.com/2023/01/31/air-force-provides-official-position-fufeng-project-grand-forks/*

92 Meghan Arbegast, *Year-long Fufeng debate comes to an end after Grand Forks council members vote to stop project,* Grand Forks Herald, (6 February 2023), *https://www.grandforksherald.com/news/local/year-long-fufeng-debate-comes-to-an-end-after-grand-forks-council-members-vote-to-stop-project*

93 Ibid., *Who is Helping the CCP Take Down America's Food Security?*

94 Ibid., *Who is Helping the CCP Take Down America's Food Security?*

95 *Protecting National Security: How the United States Government Put Our Nation at Risk by Approving the Acquisition of Smithfield Foods by Shuanghui International,* San Joaquin Agricultural Law Review, (Vol. 23 2013-2014), *https://www.sjcl.edu/images/stories/sjalr/volumes/V23N1C3.pdf*

96 Ibid., *Who is Helping the CCP Take Down America's Food Security?*

97 Marisa Herman, *China Denies It's Hoarding Food, but Facts Show Otherwise,* News-Max, (26 April 2022), *https://www.newsmax.com/platinum/china-coronavirus-variant-stockpiling-food/2022/04/26/id/1067234/; https://www.wichita.edu/academics/business/CIBA/documents/Newsmax-26April2022.pdf*

98 Ibid., *Our Supply Chain Vulnerabilities*

99 Felix Richter, *China Is the World's Manufacturing Superpower,* Statista, (May 4, 2021), *https://www.statista.com/chart/20858/top-10-countries-by-share-of-global-manufacturing-output/*

100 Sheng Hong, Yifan Jie, Xiaosong Li, and Nathan Liu, *China's chemical industry: New strategies for a new era,* McKinsey & Company, (March 20, 2019), *https://www.mckinsey.com/industries/chemicals/our-insights/chinas-chemical-industry-new-strategies-for-a-new-era*

101 Frank J. Gaffney, Dede Laugesen, and Se Hoon Kim, *China's Dream, The World's Nightmare: How the Chinese Communist Party is Colonizing and Enslaving the Planet,* CPDC, (29 July 2021), *https://www.dropbox.com/s/nhl722aiues44pt/BRI_Report_July_2021.pdf?dl=0*

102 Steven W. Mosher, *Bully of Asia: Why China's Dream is the New Threat to World Order*, Regnery, (27 November 2017), *https://www.amazon.com/Bully-Asia-China-Dream-Threat/dp/1621576965*

103 *Emperor Xi's Colonial Buildout—The Belt and Road Gambit for Enslaving the World*, Frank Gaffney with Steve Mosher, Joseph Humire, Dr. Stephen Blank, Se Hoon Kim, Christine Douglass-Williams, and Nathan Carson, CPDC, (3 November 2022), *https://presentdangerchina.org/webinar-emperor-xis-colonial-build-out-the-belt-and-road-gambit-for-enslaving-the-world/*

104 Ibid., *China's Dream, The World's Nightmare: How the Chinese Communist Party is Colonizing and Enslaving the Planet*

105 Ibid., *Emperor Xi's Colonial Buildout—The Belt and Road Gambit for Enslaving the World*

106 Francis P. Sempa, *China and the World-Island*, The Diplomat, (26 January 2019), *https://thediplomat.com/2019/01/china-and-the-world-island/*

107 Ibid., *Emperor Xi's Colonial Buildout—The Belt and Road Gambit for Enslaving the World*

108 *China Regional Snapshot: South America*, House Foreign Affairs Committee, (Updated 25 October 2022), *https://foreignaffairs.house.gov/china-regional-snapshot-south-america/*

109 *China's Network of Ports Grows in Latin America*, Diálogo Americas, Julieta Pelcastre, (23 January 2023), *https://dialogo-americas.com/articles/chinas-network-of-ports-grows-in-latin-america/*

110 *The CCP's Unrestricted Warfare in Latin America*, Frank Gaffney with Joseph Humire, Hon. Francisco Tudela, and Victor González, CPDC, (14 July 2022), *https://presentdangerchina.org/webinar-the-ccps-unrestricted-warfare-in-latin-america/*

111 Leslie Moreno Custodio, *Peru's new Chancay mega-port shakes a village to its core*, Diáglo Chino, (May 20, 2021), *https://dialogochino.net/en/infrastructure/43228-perus-chancay-mega-port-shakes-village-to-core/*

112 Ibid., *The CCP's Unrestricted Warfare in Latin America*

113 *The CCP's Belligerent 'Wolf Warrior Diplomacy'*, Frank Gaffney with Hon. Matthew Pottinger, Hon. Robert Joseph, Hon. Douglas Feith, Esq., Hon. Robert Charles, Esq., and Col. Grant Newsham, CPDC, (25 August 2022), *https://presentdangerchina.org/webinar-unrestricted-warfare-the-ccps-belligerent-wolf-warrior-diplomacy/*

114 *The CCP's Unrestricted Warfare in the Western Pacific*, Frank Gaffney with Cleo Paskal, Col. Grant Newsham (USMC Ret.), and Capt. Bill Hamblett (USN Ret.), CPDC, (7 July 2022), *https://presentdangerchina.org/webinar-the-ccps-unrestricted-warfare-in-the-western-pacific/*

115 Ibid., *The CCP's Unrestricted Warfare in the Western Pacific*

116 *Joint Statement of the Russian Federation and the People's Republic of China on the International Relations Entering a New Era and the Global Sustainable Development*, Kremlin, (4 February 2022), *http://en.kremlin.ru/supplement/5770*

117 Jeans Nyabiage, *Who benefits most from China-Russia-South Africa military drills?*, *South China Morning Post*, (4 February 2023), *https://www.scmp.com/news/ china/military/article/3209003/who-benefits-most-china-russia-south-africa-military-drills*

118 *The CCP's "No Limits Partnership" with Putin's Russia*, Frank Gaffney with J.R. Nyquist, Capt. James Fanell, (USN Ret.), Charles "Sam" Faddis, Col. John Mills, (USA Ret.), and Dr. Bradley Thayer, PhD, CPDC, (28 July 2022), *https://present-dangerchina.org/webinar-the-ccps-unrestricted-warfare-and-its-no-limits-partnership-with-putins-russia/*

119 *Cox Report, "Appendices" U.S. House of Representatives*. Archived from the original on March 9, 2014. Retrieved (December 10, 2014) *https://archive. ph/20140309085607/http://www.house.gov/coxreport/chapfs/app.html*

120 J.R. Nyquist, *Beijing's War Plan: An Interview with Lude Media*, J.R. Nyquist Blog, (4 June 2022), *https://jrnyquist.blog/2022/06/04/beijings-war-plan-an-interview-with-lude-media/*

121 Ibid., *The CCP's "No Limits Partnership" with Putin's Russia*

122 *Carien du Plessis, South Africa's Naval Exercise with Russia, China Raises Western Alarm, https://www.reuters.com/world/south-africas-naval-exercise-with-russia-china-raises-western-alarm-2023-02-17/*

123 Eric Reguly, *China's Piraeus power play: In Greece, a port project offers Beijing leverage over Europe*, *The Globe and Mail*, (7 July 2019), *https://www.theglobeandmail. com/world/article-chinas-piraeus-power-play-in-greece-a-port-project-offers-beijing/*

124 Michael Hart, *Central Asia's Oil and Gas Now Flows to the East*, *The Diplomat*, (18 August 2016), *https://thediplomat.com/2016/08/central-asias-oil-and-gas-now-flows-to-the-east/*

125 Ibid., *The CCP's Unrestricted Warfare in the Western Pacific*

126 Emily Feng, *China Celebrates Its Communist Party's Centennial With Spectacle, Saber Rattling*, NPR, (1 July 2021), *https://www.npr.org/2021/07/01/1012053737/ china-celebrates-its-communist-partys-centennial-with-spectacle-saber-rattling*

127 *The CCP is Inside our (Electrical) Wire*, Frank Gaffney with Lt. Col. Tommy Waller, Texas State Sen. Bob Hall, and Kevin Freeman, CPDC, (1 August 2022), *https:// presentdangerchina.org/webinar-unrestricted-warfare-the-ccp-is-inside-our-electrical-wire/*

128 *The Digital Gulag at Davos and the WHO: The Fight Continues*, Frank Gaffney and Reggie Littlejohn with Leo Hohmann, Steve Kirsch, David Bell, James Roguski, Jay Valentine, Hon. Pete Hoekstra, CPDC-SVPTF, (13 June 2022), *https://presentdan-*

gerchina.org/webinar-the-digital-gulag-at-davos-and-the-who-the-fight-continues/

129 *Pulling the Plug: Who's Helping the CCP to Take Down U.S. Energy Security?,* Frank Gaffney with Dr. Bradley Thayer, Dave Walsh, Lieutenant Colonel Tommy Waller, and Brian Kennedy, CPDC, (13 September 2022), *https://presentdanger-china.org/webinar-usa-betrayed-pulling-the-plug-whos-helping-the-ccp-take-down-u-s-energy-security/*

130 Matthew McMullan, *The World is Very Dependent on China for its Solar Panels, Alliance for American Manufacturing,* (13 July 2022), *https://www.americanmanu-facturing.org/blog/the-world-is-very-dependent-on-china-for-its-solar-panels/*

131 David Blackmon, *China Maintains Plans For Massive Additional Coal Expansion, Forbes,* (15 November 2022), *https://www.forbes.com/sites/davidblack-mon/2022/11/15/china-maintains-plans-for-massive-additional-coal-expansion/?sh=7f5958e22e35*

132 *Selling U.S. Strategic Oil Reserves to the CCP is Selling Out America,* Frank Gaffney with Charles "Sam" Faddis, Dave Walsh, Capt. James Fanell, USN (Ret.), and Kevin D. Freeman, CPDC, (12 July 2022), *https://presentdangerchina.org/webi-nar-selling-u-s-strategic-oil-reserves-to-the-ccp-is-selling-out-america/*

133 Andrew Ross Sorkin, Jason Karaian, Sarah Kessler, Stephen Gandel, Michael J. de la Merced, Lauren Hirsch and Ephrat Livni, *Larry Fink Defends Stakehold-er Capitalism, The New York Times,* (18 January 2023), *https://www.nytimes.com/2022/01/18/business/dealbook/fink-blackrock-woke.html*

134 Audrey Conklin, *BlackRock investments in China: Consumers' Research warning con-sumers, governments,* FOXBusiness, (2 December 2021), *https://www.foxbusiness.com/politics/blackrock-china-consumers-research-warning*

135 *The Enemies Within — Biden, Larry Fink, and Other CCP-captured Elites,* Frank Gaffney with Trevor Loudon, Will Hild, Xi Van Fleet, Peter Schweizer, Charles "Sam" Faddis, CPDC, (9 June 2022), *https://presentdangerchina.org/webinar-the-enemies-within-biden-larry-fink-and-other-ccp-captured-elites/*

136 Ibid., *Selling U.S. Strategic Oil Reserves to the CCP is Selling Out America*

137 Christopher M. Matthews and Emily Glazer, *Exxon Debates Abandoning Some of Its Biggest Oil and Gas Projects, Wall Street Journal,* (20 October 2021), *https://www.wsj.com/articles/exxon-debates-abandoning-some-of-its-biggest-oil-and-gas-projects-11634739779*

138 Brad Plumer, Lisa Friedman, Max Bearak, Jenny Gross, In a First, Rich Coun-tries Agree to Pay for Climate Damages in Poor Nations, New York Times, (19 November 2022), *https://www.nytimes.com/2022/11/19/climate/un-climate-damage-cop27.html*

139 *The CCP's Pen Pals: The U.S. Media as Enablers of America's Mortal Enemy,* Frank Gaffney with Prof. Kerry Gershaneck, Lance Crayon, Benjamin Weingarten, and

Lee Smith, CPDC, (30 August 2022), *https://presentdangerchina.org/webinar-usa-betrayed-the-ccps-pen-pals-the-u-s-media-as-enablers-of-americas-mortal-enemy/*

140 *Manchin, Cruz and Colleagues Introduce Legislation to Block Strategic Petroleum Reserve Sales to China*, Senate Committee on Energy & Natural Resources, (1 February 2023), *https://www.energy.senate.gov/2023/2/manchin-cruz-and-colleagues-introduce-legislation-to-block-strategic-petroleum-reserve-sales-to-china*

141 Ibid., *Selling U.S. Strategic Oil Reserves to the CCP is Selling Out America*

142 Ibid., *Selling U.S. Strategic Oil Reserves to the CCP is Selling Out America*

143 Ibid., *The CCP is Inside our (Electrical) Wire*

144 Kerry Breen, *North Carolina attacks underscore power grid vulnerabilities: "Destroying this infrastructure can have a crippling effect"*, CBS News, (7 December 2022), *https://www.cbsnews.com/news/north-carolina-power-grid-attack-vulnerable/*

145 *Hackers Attack Every 39 Seconds*, Security Magazine, (10 February 2017), *https://www.securitymagazine.com/articles/87787-hackers-attack-every-39-seconds*

146 Andy Greenberg, Security News This Week: Attackers Keep Targeting the US Electric Grid; Plus: Chinese hackers stealing US Covid relief funds, a cyberattack on the Met Opera website, and more, Wired, (10 December 2022), *https://www.wired.com/story/attacks-us-electrical-grid-security-roundup/*

147 Ibid., *The CCP is Inside our (Electrical) Wire*

148 *Former US Homeland chief warns Chinese solar inverters pose cyber threat*, S&P Global Market Intelligence, (6 November 2018), *https://www.spglobal.com/marketintelligence/en/news-insights/latest-news-headlines/former-us-homeland-chief-warns-chinese-solar-inverters-pose-cyber-threat-47589890*

149 Blake Sobczak and Peter Behr, *China and America's 400-ton electric albatross*, EnergyWire, (25 April 2019), *https://www.eenews.net/articles/china-and-americas-400-ton-electric-albatross/*

150 Caitlin Burke, *A Cyber Pearl Harbor': How China Built in a 'Backdoor' Threat that Could Take Down the US Electric Grid*, CBN News, (08 June 2022), *https://cmsedit.cbn.com/cbnnews/us/2021/july/the-weak-link-how-china-built-in-a-backdoor-threat-that-could-take-down-the-us-electric-grid*

151 *Executive Order on Securing the United States Bulk-Power System*, Trump White House Archives, (1 May 2020), *https://trumpwhitehouse.archives.gov/presidential-actions/executive-order-securing-united-states-bulk-power-system/*

152 *President Trump Signs Executive Order Securing the United States Bulk-Power System*, U.S. Department of Energy, (1 May 2020), *https://www.energy.gov/articles/president-trump-signs-executive-order-securing-united-states-bulk-power-system*

153 Ibid., *Pulling the Plug: Who's Helping the CCP to Take Down U.S. Energy Security?*

154 *Memorandum For Senior Pentagon Leadership: Defense Agency And DoD Field Ac-*

tivity Directors, U.S. Secretary of Defense, (5 February 2021), *https://media.defense. gov/2021/Feb/05/2002577485/-1/-1/0/STAND-DOWN-TO-ADDRESS-EX- TREMISM-IN-THE-RANKS.PDF*

155 *Biden's Takedown of America's Military,* Frank Gaffney with Lieutenant General Robert "Rod" Bishop, Captain James Fanell, Col. Robert Maness, U.S. Air Force, (Ret.), Richard Fisher, and Elaine Donnelly, CPDC, (9 August 2022), *https:// presentdangerchina.org/webinar-usa-betrayed-bidens-takedown-of-americas-military/*

156 Report on Countering Extremist Activity Within the Department of Defense, U.S. Department of Defense, (December 2021) *https://media.defense.gov/2021/ Dec/20/2002912573/-1/-1/0/REPORT-ON-COUNTERING-EXTREMIST-AC- TIVITY-WITHIN-THE-DEPARTMENT-OF-DEFENSE.PDF*

157 Roundtable on Critical Race Theory in the Military, Mike Rosen with Lt Gen Rod Bishop and STARRS VP Dr Ron Scott, Lt. Col. Matt Lohmeier, Denver's KOA 850 AM, (9 July 2021), *https://starrs.us/roundtable-on-critical-race-theory/*

158 Oriana Pawlyk, *Space Force CO Who Got Holiday Call from Trump Fired Over Com- ments Decrying Marxism in the Military,* Military.com, (15 May 2021), *https:// www.military.com/daily-news/2021/05/15/space-force-co-who-got-holiday-call- trump-fired-over-comments-decrying-marxism-military.html*

159 Ibid., *Biden's Takedown of America's Military*

160 Ray Bowden, *Exploring big ideas: Diversity and Inclusion Reading Room opens at Academy,* US Air Force Academy Public Affairs, (19 February 2021), *https:// www.usafa.af.mil/News/News-Display/Article/2508630/exploring-big-ideas-diversi- ty-and-inclusion-reading-room-opens-at-academy/*

161 Alex Horton, *Pentagon bedeviled by recruitment failures as solutions prove elusive,* Washington Post, (21 September 2022), *https://www.washingtonpost.com/nation- al-security/2022/09/21/us-military-recruiting-crisis/*

162 Stuart Scheller, *Our All-Volunteer Military Force Implodes, RealClear Defense,* (3 February 2023), *https://www.realcleardefense.com/articles/2023/02/03/our_ all-volunteer_military_force_implodes_879776.html*

163 Carly Mayberry, *Recent Data Shows 'Stunning Increase' in Serious Harm Reports in Young Healthy Pilots: Army Lt. Col. Theresa Long, Epoch Times,* (31 January 2023), *https://www.theepochtimes.com/health/recent-data-on-stunning-increase-in-serious- harm-reports-in-young-healthy-pilots-army-lt-col-theresa-long_5021392.html*

164 Ibid., *Biden's Takedown of America's Military*

165 Ryan Finnerty, *US Air Force continues cash bonuses amid multi-year pilot shortage, Flight Global,* (11 April 2022), *https://www.flightglobal.com/fixed-wing/us-air- force-continues-cash-bonuses-amid-multi-year-pilot-shortage/148238.article*

166 *War-Footing: A Top U.S. General Orders War Preparations to Deter the CCP; Will the Rest of the Military Do the Same?* Frank Gaffney with Lt. Gen. William "Jerry"

Boykin, Capt. James Fanell (USN Ret.), Col. Robert Maness (USAF Ret.), Col. Grant Newsham (USMC Ret.), Col. Derek Harvey (USA Ret.), Dr. Bradley Thayer, PhD, CPDC, (2 February 2023), *https://presentdangerchina.org/webinar-war-footing-a-top-u-s-general-orders-war-preparations-to-deter-the-ccp/*

167 Rebecca Kheel and Steve Beynon, *Inflation Bonuses Cut from Defense Bill, But Other Allowances Boosted,* Military.com, (7 December 2022), *https://www.military.com/daily-news/2022/12/07/inflation-bonuses-cut-defense-bill-other-allowances-boosted.html*

168 Ibid., *Biden's Takedown of America's Military*

169 Greg Hadley, *China Now Has More ICBM Launchers than the US,* Air & Space Forces Magazine, (7 February 2023), *https://www.airandspaceforces.com/stratcom-china-more-icbm-launchers-than-us-not-more-missiles-warheads/*

170 Gabriel Honrada, *China's hypersonic triad pressing down on US, Asia Times,* (4 February 2023), *https://asiatimes.com/2023/02/chinas-hypersonic-triad-pressing-down-on-us/*

171 The CCP 'Goes Nuclear': The Truth About Its Breakout Buildup; Experts Factfind Pentagon Report Low-balling the Growing Chinese Threat, Frank Gaffney with Dr. Mark Schneider, Richard Fisher, LtG Stephen Kwast (Ret.), Hon. Robert Joseph, Dr. Philip Karber, Dr. Matthew Kroenig, CPDC, (7 December 2022), *https://presentdangerchina.org/webinar-the-ccp-goes-nuclear-the-truth-about-its-breakout-buildup/*

172 *Does the CCP Think It Can Fight and Win a Nuclear War?; Experts Evaluate the Evidence — and the Implications — if the Answer is 'Yes',* Frank Gaffney with Richard Fisher, Mark Schneider, PhD, and Phillip Karber, PhD, CPDC, (16 February 2023), *https://presentdangerchina.org/webinar-does-the-ccp-think-it-can-fight-and-win-a-nuclear-war/*

173 Ibid., *The CCP 'Goes Nuclear': The Truth About Its Breakout Buildup; Experts Factfind Pentagon Report Low-balling the Growing Chinese Threat*

174 *Does the CCP Think It Can Fight and Win a Nuclear War?; Experts Evaluate the Evidence — and the Implications — if the Answer is 'Yes',* Frank Gaffney with Richard Fisher, Mark Schneider, PhD, and Phillip Karber, PhD, CPDC, (16 February 2023), *https://presentdangerchina.org/webinar-does-the-ccp-think-it-can-fight-and-win-a-nuclear-war/*

175 Ibid., *The CCP 'Goes Nuclear': The Truth About Its Breakout Buildup; Experts Factfind Pentagon Report Low-balling the Growing Chinese Threat*

176 *Civil-Military Fusion: The CCP's Whole-of-Society Warfare Against Us—and Americans' Enabling of It,* Frank Gaffney with Gordon G. Chang, Charles "Sam" Faddis, Col. Lawrence Sellin, Stephen Soukup, and John Guandolo, CPDC, (20 December 2022), *https://presentdangerchina.org/webinar-civil-military-fusion-the-ccps-whole-of-society-warfare-against-us/*

177 *The CCP's 'Whole-of-Society' Spying on America — Our Defense Requires No Less an Effort,* Frank Gaffney with Nicholas Eftimiades, Hon. Pete Hoekstra, Charles "Sam" Faddis, and Col. Grant Newsham, CPDC, (27 October, 2022), *https://presentdangerchina.org/webinar-unrestricted-warfare-the-ccps-whole-of-society-spying-on-america/*

178 *The CCP's Plans for an Ethnic Fifth Column?,* Frank Gaffney with Gordon G. Chang, Esq., Dr. Sasha Gong, Dr. Xiaoxu Sean Lin, and Xi Van Fleet, CPDC, (1 September 2022), *https://presentdangerchina.org/webinar-unrestricted-warfare-the-ccps-plans-for-an-ethnic-fifth-column/*

179 *The CCP's "Unrestricted Warfare" in Outer Space,* Frank Gaffney with Lieutenant General Steven Kwast, U.S. Air Force (Ret.), Brigadier General Robert Spalding, U.S. Air Force (Ret.), Dr. Greg Autry, PhD, and Richard Fisher, CPDC, (21 July 2022), *https://presentdangerchina.org/the-ccps-unrestricted-warfare-in-outer-space/*

180 *The CCP's Unrestricted Warfare in the Western Pacific,* Frank Gaffney with Cleo Paskal, Col. Grant Newsham (USMC Ret.), and Capt. Bill Hamblett (USN Ret.), CPDC, (7 July 2022), *https://presentdangerchina.org/webinar-the-ccps-unrestricted-warfare-in-the-western-pacific/*

181 Ibid., *The CCP's Unrestricted Warfare in the Western Pacific*

182 *The CCP is at War with America—What Are We Going to Do to Win?—Next Steps for Congressional Select Committee on China,* Frank Gaffney with Dr. Bradley Thayer, Peter Schweizer, Gordon G. Chang, and Brian Kennedy, CPDC, (8 November 2022), *https://presentdangerchina.org/the-ccp-is-at-war-with-america-what-are-we-going-to-do-to-win/*

183 *Seeding the Vote: China's Influence in the 2020 U.S. General Election,* CPDC, (28 November 2020), *https://presentdangerchina.org/seeding-the-vote-chinas-influence-in-the-2020-us-general-election/*

184 *Enemies Within the Church,* Filmmakers Judd Saul, Trevor Loudon, and movie host, Pastor Cary Gordon, of Cornerstone World Outreach in Sioux City, Iowa, (2021), *https://enemieswithinthechurch.com/*

185 *Formula for Fratricide: Biden's 'Othering' of MAGA,* Frank Gaffney with Dede Laugesen, Dr. Michael Rectenwald, Charles "Sam" Faddis, Trevor Loudon, and Brian Kennedy, CPDC, (7 September 2022) *https://presentdangerchina.org/webinar-usa-betrayed-formula-for-fratricide-bidens-othering-of-maga/*

186 Michael Rectenwald, *Thought Criminal,* World Encounter Institute/New English Review, (1 December 2020), *https://www.amazon.com/Thought-Criminal-Michael-Rectenwald/dp/1943003467*

187 Ibid., *Formula for Fratricide: Biden's 'Othering' of MAGA*

188 Donald J. Hanle, *Terrorism: The Newest Face of Warfare,* Potomac Books Inc., (31 January 2007), *https://www.amazon.com/Terrorism-Warfare-Donald-J-Hanle-eb-*

ook/dp/B005CWNL6Q/?pldnSite=1

189 Ibid., *Formula for Fratricide: Biden's 'Othering' of MAGA*

190 President Biden Full Speech on Democracy, C-Span, 1 Sept. 2022, *https://www. youtube.com/watch?v=JemWkV2Vcic*

191 Ibid., *Formula for Fratricide: Biden's 'Othering' of MAGA*

192 Ibid., *Formula for Fratricide: Biden's 'Othering' of MAGA*

193 *Garland defends school board memo amid Republican criticism,* AP News, 27 Oct, 2021, *https://apnews.com/article/education-violence-school-boards-merrick-garland-congress-6069cd1bf2286bcc57c62e679db6780f*

194 *Unrestricted Warfare On America's Families by the CCP and Its Friends,* Frank Gaffney with Xi Van Fleet, Reggie Littlejohn, Esq., Dr. Robert Malone, M.D., Elizabeth Yore, Esq., Lieutenant General William "Jerry" Boykin, and Sam Sorbo, CPDC, (8 September 2022), *https://presentdangerchina.org/webinar-unrestricted-warfare-on-americas-families-by-the-ccp-and-its-friends/*

195 Ibid., *Unrestricted Warfare On America's Families by the CCP and Its Friends*

196 Jared Ball , *A Short History of Black Lives Matter,* transcript of interview: Patrisse Cullors with Jared Ball, The Real News, (23 July 2015), *https://therealnews.com/pcullors0722blacklives*

197 Joshua Rhett Miller, *BLM site removes page on 'nuclear family structure' amid NFL vet's criticism,* New York Post, (24 September 2020), *https://nypost. com/2020/09/24/blm-removes-website-language-blasting-nuclear-family-structure/*

198 Snejana Farberov, *DEA seized enough fentanyl doses to kill every American in 2022,* (21 December 2022), *https://nypost.com/2022/12/21/dea-seized-enough-fentanyl-doses-to-kill-every-american-in-2022/*

199 Todd Bensman, *America's Covert Border War: The Untold Story of the Nation's Battle to Prevent Jihadist Infiltration,* (23 February 2021), *https://www.amazon.com/Americas-Covert-Border-War-Infiltration/dp/1642937258*

200 Todd Bensman, *Overrun: How Joe Biden Unleashed the Greatest Border Crisis in U.S. History,* Bombardier Books, (21 February 2023), *https://www.amazon.com/Overrun-Unleashed-Greatest-Border-History/dp/1637585705*

201 *Taking Down the Border, Taking Down America,* Frank Gaffney with Todd Bensman, Michael Yon, Trayce Bradford, and Ben Bergquam, CPDC, 4 October 2022), *https://presentdangerchina.org/webinar-usa-betrayed-taking-down-the-border-taking-down-america/*

202 *2022 was a deadly (but hopeful) year in America's opioid crisis,* NPR, 31 Dec. 2022, *https://www.npr.org/2022/12/31/1145797684/2022-was-a-deadly-but-hopeful-year-in-americas-opioid-crisis*

203 Leah MarieAnn Klett, *China makes churches replace Ten Commandments with Xi*

Jinping quotes: 'This is what the devil has always done', Christian Post, (17 September 2019), https://www.christianpost.com/news/china-makes-churches-replace-ten-commandments-with-xi-jinping-quotes-this-is-what-the-devil-has-always-done.html

204 Ibid., *Unrestricted Warfare On America's Families by the CCP and Its Friends*

205 *Religion in China,* Council on Foreign Relations, 25 Sept. 2020, https://www.cfr.org/backgrounder/religion-china

206 *Open Doors USA World Watch Report 2022,* Open Doors USA, (currently unavailable online after reorganization but available by request from Open Doors US), (6 January 2022), https://www.opendoorsus.org/

207 Ibid., *Formula for Fratricide: Biden's 'Othering' of MAGA*

208 *FBI retracts leaked document orchestrating investigation of Catholics,* Catholic News Agency, By Tyler Arnold, Joe Bukuras, 9 Feb. 2023, https://www.catholic-newsagency.com/news/253600/fbi-retracts-leaked-document-orchestrating-investiga-tion-of-catholics

209 *Enemies Within the Church,* Filmmakers Judd Saul, Trevor Loudon, and movie host, Pastor Cary Gordon, of Cornerstone World Outreach in Sioux City, Iowa, (2021), https://enemieswithinthechurch.com/

210 Ibid., *Taking Down the Border, Taking Down America*

211 *Report: Survey of Chinese Espionage in the United States Since 2000, Center for Strategic and International Studies,* (2021), https://www.csis.org/programs/strate-gic-technologies-program/archives/survey-chinese-espionage-united-states-2000

212 Ibid., *Seeding the Vote: China's Influence in the 2020 U.S. General Election*

213 *Hundreds of fake Twitter accounts linked to China sowed disinformation prior to the US election,* Cardiff University, (28 Jan. 2021), https://www.cardiff.ac.uk/news/view/2491763-hundreds-of-fake-twitter-accounts-linked-to-china-sowed-disinforma-tion-prior-to-the-us-election,-with-some-continuing-to-amplify-reactions-to-the-capitol-building-riot-report

214 Ibid., *Hundreds of fake Twitter accounts linked to China sowed disinformation prior to the US election,* Cardiff University

215 *The Carter-Baker Commission, 16 Years Later: Voting by Mail,* Rice University's Baker Institute for Public Policy, (28 April 2021), https://www.bakerinstitute.org/event/carter-baker-commission-16-years-later-voting-mail

216 *The CCP's Pen Pals: The U.S. Media as Enablers of America's Mortal Enemy,* Frank Gaffney with Prof. Kerry Gershaneck, Lance Crayon, Benjamin Weingarten, and Lee Smith, CPDC, (30 August 2022), https://presentdangerchina.org/webinar-usa-betrayed-the-ccps-pen-pals-the-u-s-media-as-enablers-of-americas-mortal-enemy/

217 Lara Jakes, Steven Lee Myers, *Tense Talks With China Left U.S. 'Cleareyed' About Beijing's Intentions, Officials Say,* New York Times, (25 March 2021), https://www.

nytimes.com/2021/03/19/world/asia/china-us-alaska.html

218 Ibid., *The CCP's Pen Pals: The U.S. Media as Enablers of America's Mortal Enemy*

219 Kerry K Gershaneck, *Political Warfare: Strategies for Combating China's Plan to "Win without Fighting"*, (30 October 2022), *https://www.amazon.com/Political-Warfare-Strategies-Combating-Fighting/dp/B08P29D3JS*

220 Kerry K. Gershaneck, *Media Warfare: Taiwan's Battle for the Cognitive Domain*, (3 October 2021), *https://www.amazon.com/Media-Warfare-Taiwans-Battle-Cognitive/dp/B09HG19F8V*

221 Ibid., *The CCP's Pen Pals: The U.S. Media as Enablers of America's Mortal Enemy*

222 *CCP buys media influence by paying millions to US dailies, magazines:* Report, *Times of India*, (4 July 2021), *https://timesofindia.indiatimes.com/world/china/ccp-buys-media-influence-by-paying-millions-to-us-dailies-magazines-report/articleshow/84109897.cms*

223 Ibid., *The CCP's Pen Pals: The U.S. Media as Enablers of America's Mortal Enemy*

224 Robert Spaulding, *Stealth War: How China Took Over While America's Elite Slept*, Portfolio, (1 October 2019), *https://www.amazon.com/Stealth-War-China-While-Americas/dp/0593084349*

225 Robert Spaulding, *War Without Rules: China's Playbook for Global Domination*, Sentinel, (19 April 2022), *https://www.amazon.com/War-Without-Rules-Playbook-Domination/dp/0593331044*

226 *TikTok Timebomb: The CCP's Virtual Weapon Platform — Growing Chorus Recognizes Addictive App as National Security Treat, Urges Ban*, Frank Gaffney with BG Robert Spalding, Connie Elliott, Col. John Mills (USA Ret.), Joe Allen. With video clips: Sens. Tom Cotton and Mark Warner, and FBI Dir. Christopher Wray, and FCC Commissioner Brandon Carr, CPDC, (22 November 2022), *https://presentdangerchina.org/webinar-tiktok-timebomb/*

227 Ibid., *TikTok Timebomb: The CCP's Virtual Weapon Platform*

228 Ibid., *TikTok Timebomb: The CCP's Virtual Weapon Platform*

229 Ibid., *TikTok Timebomb: The CCP's Virtual Weapon Platform*

230 Ibid, *TikTok Timebomb: The CCP's Virtual Weapon Platform*

231 Bobby Allyn, *Trump Signs Executive Order That Will Effectively Ban Use Of TikTok In the U.S.*, NPR, (6 August, 2020), *https://www.npr.org/2020/08/06/900019185/trump-signs-executive-order-that-will-effectively-ban-use-of-tiktok-in-the-u-s*

232 Ibid., *TikTok Timebomb: The CCP's Virtual Weapon Platform*

233 Ibid., *TikTok Timebomb: The CCP's Virtual Weapon Platform*

234 *The Abiding CCP Trojan Horses on America's Campuses,* Frank Gaffney with Dr.

Ian Oxnevad, PhD, Dr. John Lenczowski, PhD, Trevor Loudon, and Caleb Max, CPDC, (2 August 2022), *https://presentdangerchina.org/webinar-usa-betrayed-the-abiding-ccp-trojan-horses-on-americas-campuses/*

235 Rachelle Peterson, *Outsourced to China, Confucius Institutes and Soft Power in American Higher Education*, National Association of Scholars (NAS), (05 April 2017), *https://www.nas.org/reports/outsourced-to-china/full-report*

236 Rachelle Peterson, *After Confucius Institutes: China's Enduring Influence on American Higher Education*, National Association of Scholars (NAS), (15 June 2022), *https://www.nas.org/reports/after-confucius-institutes/full-report*

237 Ibid., *The Abiding CCP Trojan Horses on America's Campuses*

238 Ibid., *The Abiding CCP Trojan Horses on America's Campuses*

239 *The CCP's Not-so-secret Weapon: 'Elite Capture'*, Frank Gaffney with Steven Mosher, Peter Schweizer, Charles "Sam" Faddis, and Trevor Loudon, CPDC, (22 September 2022), *https://presentdangerchina.org/webinar-unrestricted-warfare-the-ccps-not-so-secret-weapon-elite-capture/*

240 *William Burns: Director of the Central Intelligence Agency,* AccountabilityInitiative. org, (14 April 2021), *https://accountabilityinitiative.org/william-burns-director-of-the-central-intelligence-agency/*

241 Natalie Winters, *EXPOSED: Biden's CIA Director Claims He Cut Ties with Chinese Communists, But His Group Maintains Links*, National Pulse, (30 April 2021), *https://thenationalpulse.com/2021/04/30/biden-cia-director-lied-about-ccp-ties/*

242 *The CCP's Belligerent 'Wolf Warrior Diplomacy'*, Frank Gaffney with Hon. Matthew Pottinger, Hon. Robert Joseph, Hon. Douglas Feith, Esq., Hon. Robert Charles, Esq., and Col. Grant Newsham, CPDC, (25 August 2022), *https://presentdangerchina.org/webinar-unrestricted-warfare-the-ccps-belligerent-wolf-warrior-diplomacy/*

243 Ibid., *The CCP's Belligerent 'Wolf Warrior Diplomacy'*

244 Ibid., *The CCP's Belligerent 'Wolf Warrior Diplomacy'*

245 Ibid., *China's Sharp Words in Alaska Signal Its More Confident Posture, New York Times*

246 *Lessons from Beijing's Balloon Belligerence: The CCP's Full-on Espionage, Its Wider Unrestricted Warfare and How to Respond*, Frank Gaffney with Richard Fisher, Ambassador Henry Cooper, PhD, Lt. Gen. William "Jerry" Boykin (USAF Ret.), Col. Robert Maness (USAF Ret.), Trevor Loudon, Col. John Mills (USA Ret.) CPDC, (7 February 2023), *https://presentdangerchina.org/webinar-lessons-from-beijings-balloon-belligerence/*

247 *The CCP's Belligerent 'Wolf Warrior Diplomacy'*, Frank Gaffney with Hon. Matthew Pottinger, Hon. Robert Joseph, Hon. Douglas Feith, Esq., Hon. Robert Charles, Esq., and Col. Grant Newsham, CPDC, (25 August 2022), *https://presentdangerchina.org/webinar-unrestricted-warfare-the-ccps-belligerent-wolf-warrior-diplomacy/*

248 *The CCP's Plans for an Ethnic Fifth Column?*, Frank Gaffney with Gordon G. Chang, Esq., Dr. Sasha Gong, Dr. Xiaoxu Sean Lin, and Xi Van Fleet, CPDC, (1 September 2022), *https://presentdangerchina.org/webinar-unrestricted-warfare-the-ccps-plans-for-an-ethnic-fifth-column/*

249 Bethany Allen-Ebrahimian, *Chinese Students in America: 300,000 and Counting; More Chinese students are studying in the U.S. than ever before, Foreign Policy,* (16 November 2015), *https://foreignpolicy.com/2015/11/16/china-us-colleges-education-chinese-students-university/*

250 Ryan Lucas, T*he Justice Department is ending its controversial China Initiative,* NPR, (Updated 23 February 2022), *https://www.npr.org/2022/02/23/1082593735/justice-department-china-initiative*

251 *Information About the Department of Justice's China Initiative and a Compilation of China-Related Prosecutions Since 2018,* Department of Justice, Archives, (as of 19 November 2021), *https://www.justice.gov/archives/nsd/information-about-department-justice-s-china-initiative-and-compilation-china-related*

252 *The CCP's Ominous 'Overseas Police Service Centers',* Frank Gaffney with Lieutenant General William "Jerry" Boykin, Charles "Sam" Faddis, Hon. Kenneth DeGraffenreid, Col. Dan Gallington, John Guandolo, and Hon. Robert Charles, Esq., CPDC, (6 October 2022), *https://presentdangerchina.org/webinar-unrestricted-warfare-the-ccps-ominous-overseas-police-service-centers/*

253 *230,000 Chinese "persuaded to return" from abroad, China to establish Extraterritoriality,* Investigations, Safeguard Defenders, (12 September 2022), *https://safeguarddefenders.com/en/blog/230000-policing-expands*

254 Ibid., *The CCP's Ominous 'Overseas Police Service Centers'*

255 Andrew Thornebrooke, *Secret CCP Overseas Police Station in NYC Closed After Reported FBI Raid, Epoch Times,* (2 February 2023), *https://www.theepochtimes.com/secret-ccp-overseas-police-station-in-nyc-shutdown-after-reported-fbi-raid_5029711.html*

256 Ibid., *The CCP's Ominous 'Overseas Police Service Centers'*

257 Ibid., *The CCP's Ominous 'Overseas Police Service Centers'*

258 *Designate the Chinese Communist Party as a Transnational Criminal Organization,* CPDC, (7 July 2021), *https://presentdangerchina.org/designate-the-chinese-communist-party-as-a-transnational-criminal-organization/*

259 Select Committee on the Strategic Competition Between the United States and the Chinese Communist Party, Clerk of the United States House of Representatives, *https://clerk.house.gov/committees/ZS00*

260 CPDC Events & Webinars Videos, CPDC, (2019-2023), *https://presentdangerchina.org/category/videos/cpdc-events-and-webinars-video/*

Index